WHY DID SHE JUMP?

WHY DID SHE JUMP?

My Daughter's Battle with Bipolar Disorder

JOAN E. CHILDS, LCSW

Health Communications, Inc.
Deerfield Beach, Florida

www.hcibooks.com

**Library of Congress Cataloging-in-Publication Data
is available through the Library of Congress**

© 2014 Joan E. Childs

ISBN-13: 978-07573-1697-5 (Paperback)
ISBN-10: 07573-1697-2 (Paperback)
ISBN-13: 978-07573-1698-2 (ePub)
ISBN-10: 07573-1698-0 (ePub)

Publisher: Health Communications, Inc.
      3201 S.W. 15th Street
      Deerfield Beach, FL 33442–8190

Cover photo © Joan E. Childs
Cover design by Larissa Hise Henoch
Interior design and formatting by Lawna Patterson Oldfield

To my daughter, Pamela.

May your beautiful soul rest in peace forever.

1963–1998

ACKNOWLEDGMENTS

I am deeply grateful to those who've supported me while writing this book. I want to thank Dr. Arnold Lieber for his assistance in providing accurate psychiatric terminology and medical editing. My sincere appreciation to Pamela Wilder for her painstaking efforts in integrating the preliminary editing and for her patience with my technical incompetence. I am thankful to all of my family and friends who gave their time and attention to reading the manuscript to make sure the presentation of facts, as seen through my eyes and experiences, was accurate.

I greatly appreciate the editing that was provided to me by Allison Janse and Erin Brown—for their time and talent—and to Health Communication, Inc. for their willingness to publish my story.

Most of all, I want to express my gratitude to John Gibbons, who passed away in 2012. Confident that this book might provide help to others with similar circumstances and experiences, he helped make this publication possible by believing in me. If my story helps just one person who has suffered the loss and grief of a loved one through suicide or mental illness, then his support has been worthwhile.

CONTENTS

PREFACE

August 2, 1998

Oprah Winfrey
The Oprah Winfrey Show
110 N. Carpenter St.
Chicago, Illinois 60607

Falling Through the Cracks

Dear Oprah,

On July 2, the same morning your show featured Bipolar Disorder, my thirty four-year-old daughter leaped to her death from the window of her father's fifteen-story apartment. Although many psychiatrists had diagnosed Pam with Bipolar I Disorder, I believe a major contributing cause of her death was our ineffective, dysfunctional health system.

I call it the HMO tragedy.

A PhD psychologist and a clinical social worker, Pam had been a therapist for many years specializing in Inner Child Work at the John Bradshaw Center. Mr. Bradshaw has also been featured on your program several times. After moving back to Florida from California a few years ago, she continued to seek treatment with many different psychologists and psychiatrists who were unable to help her mainly because there was no responsive, supportive, in-patient facility available under her HMO.

Her father, a physician, and I, a clinical social worker, helped to finance her medical needs until they became too excessive for our combined resources. Even when we tried to extend ourselves financially for the help she so desperately needed, we were denied or dismissed. She did not meet the criteria for in-patient treatment.

She was hospitalized briefly several times just long enough for stabilization, but never long enough for effective and optimum results. Each time we were given the same response: she didn't meet the criteria for long-term care. Her HMO physicians denied hospitalization many times, stating that she did not appear to be harmful to herself or others. These were the times we elected to hospitalize her under the care of a physician "not on the plan." These were the times we paid out of pocket for the care denied to her by her HMO. However, even with private extended hospitalization, the results were the same—insufficient and short term.

Her illness quite often disguised its own implications. Along with all her physicians, many of whom were "not on the plan," we tried unsuccessfully to place her in a safe environment where she could receive proper treatment until she was safely stabilized. We learned, after much time, effort, and expense that no such environment existed for the middle class.

We then pursued the governmental Medicaid/disability route, which, by the time she passed away, had been in process for more than three years. Every time she followed up, various bureaucrats advised her that her "application was in process" and could offer no other information.

Bipolar I Disorder can cause both physical and emotional paralysis. My beautiful, intelligent, loving daughter went from being a vivacious, gifted, productive woman to a terrorized, dysfunctional, regressive, and helpless little girl. Everyone who knew her both personally and professionally was both blessed and touched by the encounter. She literally transformed the lives of her patients. John Bradshaw would say she was a "wizard" therapist.

Her story must be told, not because she is my daughter, but because she is OUR daughter. Suicide took the lives of 29,350 Americans in 2000. Statistics reveal that more people die from suicide than from homicide. Overall, suicide is the eleventh leading cause of death for young people aged fifteen to twenty-four. Approximately 1 in 83 or 3.3 million people in the United States have suffered interminably from Bipolar Disorder.

It was not Pam who chose death; it was the illness and its insidious invasion of her mind that made the choice. Pam would never have been capable of such a heinous decision. She loved her parents. She loved her four siblings. She loved her friends and patients. And, most of all, she cherished life.

Mental illness doesn't reveal itself as clearly as physiological disorders. There are no lab tests, X-rays, MRI's, or sophisticated technology that can determine accurate diagnosis and treatment. Most diagnoses are made from clinical interviews, and because many mental disorders often overlap in their symptoms (comorbidity), it is often difficult to diagnose precisely.

Psychotropic medication is still a "hit and miss" art form that most often doesn't effect change as precisely as do the antibiotics, inflammatory medications, and other chemical drugs used for most ailments and diseases. Unfortunately, of all the organs in the human body, science knows least about the brain. We're still in the "play around with it" stage; meaning if a medication isn't effective and does not produce results, clinicians increase the dosage, change the medication or time of ingestion, and/or combine it with another. Often, these medications do more harm than good and create a big price to pay for its ingestion. The side effects can often be as devastating as the disorder.

Since the inception of managed care, most psychiatrists have been reduced to glorified pharmacists. Insurance benefits do not cover adequately the time a patient needs to be treated properly. The listening and counseling is passed along to the therapists allowing limited visits, too limited to provide adequate care. Too often, the right hand doesn't know what the left hand is doing.

Patients with an active Bipolar I Disorder, such as Pam had, must be in a supportive, controlled environment. Even as productive participants of the healing profession, her father and I were unable to secure an appropriate facility for our daughter despite our resources. Her HMO certainly did not provide such a place.

Maybe she would have died anyway. Perhaps the illness had pre-determined and dictated her destiny. However, we wanted a real chance to save her from this wretched disaster.

The funeral chapel was filled to capacity. There was standing room only as her friends and relatives continued to pour in from all over the country as we said our last good-byes to Pam. We were all stunned. I kept wondering how a country that stands for life, liberty, and the pursuit of happiness could be so inept in caring for my daughter. How many others had fallen through the cracks?

This is not a story about a destitute, homeless, indigent, or underprivileged human being. They at least have a chance for survival. The state provides somewhat limited care, but offers an opportunity to get into the mental health system. If it had not been for the fact that Pam had a family, she would have been homeless. Nor is this a story about the rich and famous. They can survive through their own resources. This is a story about most of us. It is a story about a gifted, young woman of middle-class America whose life was lost because our system failed to do its part. Your viewers will recognize her. They will know her. Each of them has a family member, friend, or child who may be subject to this travesty. Many have already been.

One of the worst crimes in America is the HMO/managed care tragedy. With all the rhetoric and promises made, the government still does not provide effective health care. We need managed care, not managed money. How can a country that is so rich in resources, so concerned about the health and welfare of its citizens, and ostensibly the richest country in the world, be so negligent and irresponsible in its response to the health needs of Americans?

I don't have the answer. I am only one voice in America. You, Oprah, are the voice of the people. Perhaps you can present a program illustrating better models of health care. Perhaps just knowing there are answers out there can give hope for solutions. I don't want to give another example of a personal tragedy as a result of a pathetic health system. You have already effectively illustrated that. I want to advocate for a change. I am hoping that you can help. It would make my daughter's life more meaningful and her death a wake-up call and lesson for us all. Perhaps it might even save others.

Sincerely yours,
Joan E. Childs

Cc: *The Miami Herald*
The White House, Hillary Clinton
Senators Bob Graham and Connie Mack
Congresswoman Elaine Bloom

This is where my story began.

I was raw from the grief and loss, hardly able to think of anything other than my daughter. My fingers touched the keyboard with my soul's instruction. I had nothing to do but show up at the computer. My heart wrote my story.

INTRODUCTION

On July 2, 1998, my daughter Pam, a beautiful thirty-four-year old woman and gifted clinical psychologist, who had been married more than a year, killed herself. She fought for years to recover from a mental illness known as bipolar I disorder. This is her story and mine.

One expects to lose a parent to death, not a child. It's unnatural. When one loses a child, no matter what the cause or age, it leaves a deep hole in the soul, a wound that never completely heals. Time helps, but we're never quite the same.

The grief process has been torturous and unyielding. I am not sure if I will ever get closure. Some events in life are too painful to close. The pain is a reminder of the love we once shared. But perhaps closure is not necessary to heal. Perhaps healing can accommodate imperfection. Perhaps the best we can do is to remember what we had and not what we lost.

Author Leon Bouy once said, "Man has places in his heart which do not yet exist, and into them enters suffering in order that they may have existence." Pain, suffering, anger, sadness, sorrow, despair, acceptance, letting go, and moving on are all part of the task. Each of us must cope with grief in our own way. There is no right way. Time helps; caring, supportive friends help; talking helps; and counseling helps. But the pain of loss never really goes away. The emotional scars stay forever. As time passes, we must make a choice between being a victim or being a survivor. The decision may determine how you live the rest of your life.

You are reading this book for your own reasons. Perhaps you have lost a child or a loved one to suicide, a long-term illness, or sudden, unexpected death; maybe you know someone else who has experienced such a tragedy. You may even wonder if suicide makes the loss more tragic than loss from an accidental death, murder, or natural causes.

Maybe you want to understand more about the dreadful bipolar disorder (once labeled manic-depressive illness) that has a lifetime prevalence of 2.6 percent of our general population.

Whatever your reason, come with me on this personal journey through my daughter's battle with it. Perhaps my experiences will answer some of your questions, address some of your concerns, relieve some of your apprehensions, and even comfort you. Writing this book was a catharsis, a chance to sublimate and channel some of the interminable pain and grief into something constructive that might help other survivors.

This is the story of my loss, my grief, and my daughter's struggle with bipolar I disorder. It was not an easy story to write because it made everything real, and I was not sure that I was ready to cope with this reality. But I wrote it in hopes of healing myself and helping others who have experienced similar affliction.

The loss of a loved one and the ensuing grief can and often will precipitate post-traumatic stress disorder (PTSD). Although our brains are capable of intellectualizing the concept of death, the emotional part of the brain handles that loss in a separate fashion. We operate from three different regions of the brain: the *neocortex*, the *mammalian*, and the *reptilian*. This tripartite system, known as the triune brain, has independent functions. Each part responds independently and quite differently to the same stimuli. The neocortex governs the rational part of the mind. It is the most recently developed part of the brain. Not unlike a computer, it responds logically and analytically to stimuli. It asks the question: "Is it logical, reasonable, and rational?" This is the part of the mind that forms conclusions and resolutions intellectually. When someone close to us dies, the neocortex gives rational answers to our questions. This does not preclude our wondering if there was something we could have done that might have produced a different outcome; however, resolution and acceptance are somewhat easier in natural death than in suicide. In suicide, the neocortex doesn't stand a chance.

The mammalian part of the brain, the seat of emotion, takes over. It cannot compute reason or logic. It asks: "Is it painful or pleasurable?" Human beings forge toward pleasure and away from pain. The mind is flooded with a plethora of emotions that obliterate all logic and reason, closing off any access to the neocortex and rational reasoning. Shock, grief, and guilt overwhelm us and become pervasive. It is not possible to analyze. In fact, our thinking is often impaired. This is why it is essential in the grief process and recovery to acknowledge these emotions, for repression of feelings to avoid pain only postpones the inevitable and can cause more traumas later.

The reptilian part hosts the instinctual and habitual drives and asks: "Is it safe? Will I survive?" When we are thrust into a reality that we cannot comprehend or find too difficult to process, we move toward this part of our minds. Fight or flight is the common response. We either run from the situation or face it head-on. In grief and loss, facing it head-on usually is not an option because our emotional shock absorbers are instantaneous. They help us to numb out from the trauma. The purpose of the reptilian brain is to keep us safe and help us survive.

The taking of one's life is often considered unjustifiable, an abominable sin, and a deliberate violation of God's will, religion, and nature. It's thought of as an act of one's own volition as if there was a conscious choice. This is not always the case. Quite often, it is the mental illness (such as acute depression or bipolar disorder), which insidiously and relentlessly invades and fractures the mind, that makes the decision, not the person.

This is what I believe happened to Pam, who plunged fifteen stories to her death three months prior to her thirty-fifth birthday. I do not believe it was her conscious decision to do this, for she valued life as her most precious gift. The disease became her executioner. It had a life force of its own, controlling her will, her actions, and causing her death.

Pam's struggle with her demons had been going on much longer than any of her family, friends, or coworkers realized. Fearing we would make judgments, she suffered mostly in silence because she knew that we would have difficulty accepting and understanding her belief system. As a trained clinical psychologist, Pam knew how preposterous her belief system sounded to others, not unlike some psychotic patients she treated and often referred to psychiatrists for medication.

When she did share her thoughts and beliefs with us, all we could do was try to reason with her, hoping to bring her back to her senses by alleviating her fears. We tried to be sympathetic and supportive, but none of us could fight the demonic force that resided in her mind, dictating the course of her events. Nor could her psychiatrists, numerous psychologists, colleagues, friends, rabbis, priests (both Christian and Muslim), and spiritual healers, including channel psychics, shamans, a Qigong master, as well as a series of fortune tellers, psychics, and demon chasers in addition to a multitude of psychotropic medications. The demons grew larger in time—invading her dreams, convoluting her thoughts, and sucking her spirit out of her body like a vampire devouring its victim's life force. This is why I know suicide was not her conscious choice. Rather, it was the manipulation and delusionary demand of the demons that possessed her mind and sentenced her to death. Her destiny was no longer her own. She fell into a trance reinforced by

the hallucinations of her psychosis. Like the mythological Perse-
phone (daughter of the Greek goddess Demeter), Pam, too, was
abducted into the abyss, but for Pam it was forever.

Six months before she died, Pam and I met a young woman in
Israel who wrote to me after she learned about Pam's death. She
had met us in her aunt's home at a Sabbath dinner we had attended.
In an effort to console me, she wrote that her rabbi had informed
her that according to the Kabbalah (Jewish mysticism), before
we are born, we already know our destiny. God informs us of our
future. The map of our lives are disclosed, both our fortunes and
misfortunes. We choose life, knowing what the future holds in spite
of any adversity that lies ahead. She said that before I was born, I
had known that I would have a firstborn daughter whom I would
lose early, yet I chose life anyway. She said that Pam had made the
same choice, knowing full well her ill-fated destiny.

I don't claim to have any answers. I still ask why. Why was such
a young, gifted, and loving woman called to death in such a violent
manner? Why did she jump? What happened inside her mind in
that fatal moment that caused her to leap to her death? I don't
believe the rabbis or any clergy have the answers either. Perhaps
no answers can console, make sense, or help us to understand.

It is comforting to believe that our destinies are written before
we arrive, that this journey to earth is only a partial journey, and
that we are summoned home. Perhaps each of us has a mission,
and when it is fulfilled in the eyes of our creator, we go home.
This, however, does not seem relevant to the truncated lives of

little children who had no chance to follow their bliss, or to the newborns who have not yet even taken their first breath. It doesn't make sense when applied to people who spend their whole lives giving nothing to the world except pain and grief. I can only have faith and believe in a greater kingdom than the one we know. This doesn't explain why Pam struggled with such an insidious, insufferable, mental illness. It just as well might have been a fatal accident, physical illness, or chronic disability. I would like to believe that her struggle with bipolar disorder allowed her to reach out to the tormented souls of others who suffered the same. Was it this curse that gave her the blessing of empathy and insightfulness to help those who struggled with mental illness? If so, it was a double-edged sword.

I prefer to believe that God chose my daughter to do his work. As a therapist, she effected change in people that made a difference in their lives. Her patients, colleagues, teachers, and friends have confirmed this. I believe that because she was so divinely gifted, God needed her to go home to help him with much more important work—work that neither you nor I can imagine or understand. This may sound mystical. I may be going out on a limb to justify cause and find answers. I've worked in the field of psychotherapy for thirty-seven years and have learned that nothing is for sure. I am not about to launch a journey to discover answers where there may not be any. I cannot assume to know the unknowable or solve the unsolvable. I am not a self-proclaimed healer, visionary, or guru who knows the path for others or myself with any certainty or of a promise for a better life. I want to heal from the loss of my child, but I never want to forget the impact that Pam made on the lives she touched and changed, including my own. This is a better world because of the contributions Pam made to others. This is a sweeter world for the love she gave so graciously. This is a kinder world for the generosity of time and energy she offered of herself to those in need. She modeled holiness without sanctification from any organized religious order. She was religious in her being, which is more than any religion can teach or preach. Only those who do God's work according to his standards qualify as angels.

I feel honored and privileged to have been the mother of an angel.

PART I

‿◦‿◦‿◦‿

1

THE DAY MY ANGEL SAID GOOD-BYE

July 2, 1998

We often wish we could rewrite our own histories. As we reflect upon our lives, we consider the choices we made, our regrets, and all the what-ifs. If I could rewrite a part of my life, it would be the week before my daughter Pam took her life.

In March 1998, a few months before her death, I met Jim on an Internet dating service. We developed a virtual relationship, and a few months later we met in South Florida, my home. I invited him to spend the month of July with me in Beech Mountain, North Carolina, and, if things worked out, to join me in Santa Fe, New Mexico, in August while I attended a conference, a trip I'd planned a few months before I met him.

My two other daughters, Monica and Erika, were to be in North Carolina at the same time. Jim and I planned to meet them there after spending some time at his home in Wisconsin. They'd rented a cabin with some friends not too far away from mine. Pam wanted to go as well, but I thought it best for her to stay closer to home where her psychiatrist could monitor her. She would stay with her father and his girlfriend. Although unhappy about this arrangement, she acquiesced.

Truth be told, we all needed a break from the toll her illness had taken on us. We were exhausted from the relentless attention she needed.

Over time, Pam's illness had deteriorated, sending her into the depths of despair and resulting in irrational thoughts and behaviors. She fervently believed that everyone who loved and cared for her was really an agent of the Devil. In her delusional state, Pam believed that the Devil was her perpetrator, whose mission was to seize her soul. She envisioned her husband morph into a vampire. She visualized demons around me, which frightened her so that she could no longer live with me, so she fled to her sisters' home. In her lucid moments, she would cry and apologize to me for the hallucinations she could not control. Her sisters, both younger, were at a loss to know how to care for her. They would call me in horror. "Please, Mommy, you have to get her help!"

Separated from her husband, Kevin, she had a boyfriend, Barry, an orthodox Jew who with his love and devotion as well as his passion for Judaism tried hard to help her, to get her to embrace Torah, believing that God, in all his goodness and mercy, would help her heal. He brought her into his religious community, the Chabad, where he tried so earnestly to engage her with their support. Barry and Pam had met during her darkest hours, the last year of her life. She was desperate to find God and he thought he could show her the way. She had begun a new life with him, despite still being married. In her desperation, she eventually bonded with him and his religious community. He was earnest, and although someone she would have never been interested in prior to her illness, he became her teacher, friend, and lover. As her mentor, he tried to reeducate her about her Jewish faith. He tried to help her find clarity and hope. He taught her to pray, and encouraged her to reestablish a connection with Judaism. He was persistent and coached her relentlessly. It was evident to all of us that he loved Pam, and, without malice, he capitalized on his intentions. She was weak and emotionally hollow; he was devoted to her salvation. However, a few months before she passed away, she had become frightened of him and misinterpreted Barry's eagerness and love as manipulation and control. When she began to slip deeper into her illness, paranoia kicked in, and it wasn't long before she aligned him and his community with the dark side. She turned away from him and his efforts. In lucid moments, she would confess that she realized how sick she was in keeping a relationship so foreign and detrimental to her ego and selfhood.

In the beginning when Barry first brought her into his community, she was happy to be there. It seemed to offer her a sense of safety and support. As her illness progressed, she became mistrustful of both him and his community, believing they, like the others, were instruments of the Devil, too. He lost her to her illness. Leaving Barry, she fled to her sister's home. She refused to come live with me as she was sure that demons surrounded me. Even her closest friends, siblings, father, psychiatrists, and therapists became suspect to her. She became fearful and terrorized. She remained convinced that her soul was being stalked by the Devil and she doubted our sincerity and challenged our reasoning with tormented thoughts of her own.

In the beginning, her first response was that she had been chosen as a mediator between God and the Devil to resolve good and evil. In addition, she believed that the Devil was going to take her soul. She felt she had done things in her life that were irreparable; so evil, that she could not be saved.

With all my resources as a psychotherapist, with all my colleagues and extensive psychiatric network, I was unable to find a reliable in-patient facility to care for her. She eventually turned to us, her family, for protection and shelter. We had all shared this responsibility over several months, to such an extent that caregiving became a full-time job. Our lives were entangled with her illness as we tried but failed to make her feel safe. Her reality became our worst nightmares as we watched her dive deeper into the darkness of a psychotic state where none of us could reach her. Our lives became unmanageable, without hope or promise for a cure.

There was a time when she insisted that she had demons invading her. She pleaded with me to find a "demon chaser." My girlfriend, who was married to a Qi Gong Master, specialized in demon chasing. I had never heard of such a thing, except in horror films. Pam was convinced his approach would work. He worked in West Palm Beach, so her father and I hesitantly drove her there while she attended a session. We both waited in a nearby shopping mall until she was finished. When we picked her up after her session, she looked pale and frightened.

"How did it go? I asked.

"It was okay, I guess, but I still feel their presence within."

Her response was that the demons were stronger than his healing powers, so she lacked faith in his efforts.

When she became engaged the first time to Josef, her fiancé did not have money to buy her a ring, so against my mother's advice, I gave her my three-caret, pear-shaped, diamond ring that had been given to me by my first fiancé. In those days, diamonds were not as expensive as they are now. She wanted to change the setting so it would look like a new ring. I told her she could do whatever she wanted but that I expected her to pass it on to her firstborn son, so it would remain in the family. If she had no sons, she was to promise to give it to the firstborn son of any of my other children. My mother had kept vigil over this ring, holding it in a safety deposit box since I was twenty years old. I explained to Pam its value and importance. It would become an heirloom. She admitted to me, after several inquiries about the missing ring upon her and Josef's breakup, that she had lost it. She apologized profusely, but in my mind, I always felt she pawned it to help pay her traffic and parking tickets. I will never know.

Anyone living with someone with severe bipolar disorder knows that the caregivers become helpless because the patient is always unpredictable and overwhelming in their behaviors. They don't respond to reasoning, often becoming aggressive and irrational. The effort all of us had to put into reasoning and explaining things to her drained us. She needed a constant sense of safety: to be held, touched, affirmed, and reassured that she wasn't going to prison or hell. We were consistently challenged to explain the meanings of her thoughts, her delusional assumptions, and ideas of reference.

Another time there was some irrelevant incident that she challenged Erika about. She appeared annoyed about a small issue, something to do with the kitchen. She had been wearing an ingenuous smile when suddenly, without warning, she became explosive, banging on the door to Erika's room, screaming at the top of her lungs.

"You're lying to me. You're lying. You're part of this too. I can't trust you; my own sister!"

Monica related that she had to keep vigil over Pam when it came to taking her meds. An argument would prevail with Pam being noncompliant in taking her pills. Pam was convinced they were contaminated by the Devil. Her refusal to comply drained Monica, who felt exhausted by her futile efforts.

Another incident occurred when Pam was moving into her sisters' townhouse from Barry's residence. Pam needed boxes to pack her belongings. Monica, not wanting to enable her sister, requested that Pam be the one to go to Publix to see if they had any boxes. When Pam called information for their number, she was automatically connected to the store. This caused a fury within Pam. She believed that the phone call had been intercepted by the Devil. She hung up the phone and dialed the number information had given her, only to have Publix still on the line, thus reinforcing her belief that the Devil had taken action.

She pleaded with Monica to hold her during the night so she would feel protected from the Devil's entry. Monica was the only one she seemed to trust at this time. The burden was heavy and caused Monica interminable exhaustion and stress.

So often Pam would become verbally abusive, or regress into an infantile state, either crying relentlessly or having temper tantrums for no known reason any of us could surmise. I recall a time when our entire family, including her father's girlfriend, Astrid, were having dinner in a popular deli in North Miami Beach. For no apparent reason, Pam became cantankerous with me. Her language became abusive and her tone loud and offensive, to the point where I finally had to leave the restaurant in dismay, just to protect myself. The next week, she was apologetic and loving, asking for forgiveness. Her moods were unstable. She was very labile.

While she worked in my office after she returned from California, she grew hostile and impatient with my relationship with a colleague who worked with me. She would often burst into my office while I was talking with him, challenging my relationship with him and alleging that I made him more important than her. She accused me of stealing her money, alleging that I was trying to undermine her success; money she earned from clients that I had referred to her. My secretary would often be startled by her inexplicable behaviors in front of the clients who were in the waiting room to be seen by other therapists. She also accused my secretary of crediting the money she earned to me instead of her. This was during the time she was living with Kevin prior to their marriage.

Her relationship with Kevin was a nightmare. She would often leave him for days, and none of us would know her whereabouts. Kevin seemed relieved that she was gone. He never communicated much with me, but I tried to be supportive of him during this critical time.

Unable to maintain her clinical practice and incapable of working, Pam moved back and forth between my apartment and Monica and Erika's townhouse for many months. Her depression increased, but we were not aware of the implications and possible consequences. I had not considered Pam suicidal until the week I left Miami to join Jim at his home in Wisconsin. I needed to reassure myself that she was in no danger of harming herself. I called her at her father's house on Tuesday, June 30, 1998, the day before we were to drive to North Carolina. "How's it going, honey?"

"You know, Mom. One day at a time. It's a struggle, but I pray a lot."

"Are you seeing the doctor this week?" I already knew the answer.

"Yes, on Thursday." I heard the melancholy in her voice. "I miss you. I miss you so much, Mom. I wish I was there with you and my sisters."

I shared her disconsolation. "I miss you, too, sweetheart. But I think you need to be where you are safe. Daddy is with you, and we are only a phone call away." I tried to reassure her. Perhaps I was trying to reassure myself.

"I know. But it's so hard." She broke into tears.

Then I asked her the question I never wanted to ask. I closed my eyes and prayed for the answer I wanted to hear. "Are you having any bad thoughts? Are you feeling suicidal, Pam?" I held my breath as I waited for her response.

"Mom," she said lovingly, "you know what a burden I've been on you and Daddy and everyone in the family these past two years. I could never leave a legacy of suicide to those I love most in this world. And besides, you know I fear the Devil taking my soul. Why would I give it to him?" She paused. "And anyway, it's against my religion. Jews are not allowed to commit suicide."

She managed to almost convince me that she would be safe, but I had a nagging feeling in my gut that I could be wrong. I called her psychiatrist as soon as we hung up. I had met with her and Pam the week before. I asked her if she felt Pam was suicidal.

"She's psychotic, but not suicidal," she said. But I wasn't reassured, it just didn't feel right, nor did it satisfy my intuition. It seemed too likely that psychosis could precipitate suicide. I tried to dismiss the morbid thought, but it wouldn't go away.

"But what if she has a delusionary demand? What if she hears voices that tell her to jump out of a window or something equally as crazy?" I asked.

Pam knew how to disguise how ill she really was. She'd managed to fool the professionals, as well as her family. We were easy to deceive, as we never really wanted to believe she was so ill as to take her own life. Denial prevented us from being objective. The times she visited me and sat alone on my balcony on the twelfth floor made me uneasy. I would ask her to come inside to ease my discomfort. I never gave that feeling a cause, for it would have been too alarming to acknowledge.

The psychiatrist agreed to hospitalize her if she had any doubt at her next session, which was scheduled only two days later. She advised me that Pam did not meet her HMO's criteria for hospitalization. Pam needed to demonstrate that she might be harmful to herself or others, because psychosis alone would not qualify her for admittance.

"It doesn't matter!" I said. "We'll pay out of pocket. Her father and I want her to be safe. Whatever the cost, we'll take care of it. We did it before and we'll do it again."

I continued my plans to meet Jim at his home in Wisconsin. Monica was to drive my car from Miami to North Carolina so I would have a way home prior to my flying to Santa Fe for the conference. Jim and I drove together in his Ford Explorer from Wisconsin to Beech Mountain, accompanied by his chocolate Labrador, Maggie.

It was a difficult journey. We were on the road for only two days, but it seemed like twenty. We were exhausted from the drive and frustrated with the delays caused by traffic, detours, and highway construction. We were eager to reach the chalet and get out of the Explorer, which smelled like a kennel by now. Before going to the cabin, we had to stop by the rental office to pick up the key. By then it was dark and the fog was thick and heavy, making it difficult to see the hairpin curves on the steep mountain road.

When we finally arrived at the rental office, it was after midnight and pitch-black outside. We parked the car as close as possible to the front of the building as to shine the headlights on the porch so we could see. We had expected to find the keys and directions to our chalet, but there taped on the front door was a large manila envelope with a note written in bold, handwritten letters:

Call Dr. Glassman or Marlene immediately. You have an emergency. Your car is at the police station and your keys are with the dispatcher.

Marlene was my secretary and I wondered why her name was on the envelope. Dr. Glassman was my ex-husband and the father of my five children.

I panicked; something terrible had happened. Why was my car at the police department? Why were they holding my keys? Fear and confusion filled me. Then I thought perhaps something had happened to Monica while driving up from Miami. Did she have an accident? Was she injured, arrested, or even killed? Did something happen to Pam? The questions came so quickly that they flooded my mind with unspeakable thoughts. I was besieged with worry and fear.

With some difficulty, Jim and I found our way to the local police station where we learned that they didn't have my car or my keys. I asked if I could use their phone, but they refused and directed me to a public phone outside. I stepped into the booth. My hands trembled as I reached for the receiver. Holding it tightly in my hand, I dialed my ex-husband's number. My heart knew the answer, but I didn't want to hear it.

"Don't give me any bad news," I said as soon as I heard his voice.

"I'm going to give you the worst news you'll ever hear in your whole life." His voice was loud and pressured. He spoke the words that would change my life forever: "Pami killed herself this morning." He burst into uncontrollable sobbing. He was incoherent at times, riveting with sounds of shock and despair that shook the ground I stood on.

I don't remember much after that, for I too was in shock and disbelief. I collapsed into the arms of a man I hardly knew; suddenly he seemed like a stranger. I can recall screaming but I don't remember if the screams were mine, her father's, or just imagined.

My body seemed to split off from my mind, and I felt heat growing within me, like a high fever. The burning started with my ears, then invaded my throat, and radiated into my chest. My head felt swollen and hot. A sharp pain pierced my body as if a sword had been plunged into my skull and had come out through my stomach. Everything seemed like a bad dream from which I could not awaken. That moment of truth, hearing that she had leaped out of the window of her father's fifteenth-story apartment, reverberated over and over again like a video stuck in a loop. My world began to crumble. My sanity felt challenged and impaired. Nothing would ever again be the same.

It seemed that I was the last to learn about Pam's death. The journey from Wisconsin had kept me far away from the news. While traveling for two days to Beech Mountain, I had been distracted by an onslaught of country music, at least one hundred refrains of Bob Dylan, the anticipation of a new relationship, and a foul-smelling Ford Explorer. Pam had been dead for more than twelve hours by the time we reached Beech Mountain. My family had no way to reach me.

I don't know how I managed to locate the rented cabin in the dark, mountainous terrain. My mind seemed barely connected to my body. But something beyond my conscious awareness guided me to the last cabin on the road.

The phone was ringing as we entered the unfamiliar cabin. It was pitch-dark and I fumbled frantically for a light switch. Not knowing where the phone was, I followed the sound into what seemed to be the master bedroom. Before I could bring the phone to my ear, I heard my daughter Monica sobbing on the other end of the receiver; sorrow-laden with grief unlike anything I had ever heard before.

"Mommy, Mommy, Pami is dead. She's dead! My sister is dead!" she screamed over and over.

I held the phone to my ear, but could not find the words I needed to comfort her. The burning in my throat stifled my vocal chords. I finally managed to loosen my throat enough to mumble, "I know. I know." The visceral image of Pam leaping out the window obscured everything else. I heard my other daughter, Erika, howling in the background like a wounded animal. The screams went on and on as if they were trying to drown out the truth.

"No, no, no, no. It can't be. It can't be," Monica cried. "Say it isn't so. Please, please, say it isn't so."

The wailing and screaming continued for what seemed interminable. I just listened, frozen and mesmerized by their grief. I heard their screams. I heard their anguish. But that haunting image of my daughter plunging to her death was overwhelming; I stood as if frozen in a moment in time. I felt helpless to make it go away. I was powerless to change what had happened. I seemed to slip into an abyss. I felt a paralysis enter my body, penetrating my limbs, muscles, and even my cells. The heat became pervasive. It seemed to swallow me. I began to disassociate. I saw myself move away from myself.

I heard the girls say that they were coming over. The cabin they had rented was about twenty-five miles from Beech Mountain.

They asked for directions. As if an internal switch had flipped, I was back again. I was coherent. I gave them the directions, asked them how long it would take them to get there, and then reassured them that I would be fine. I told them to drive slowly, take their time, and arrive safely. I regained my composure. and by the time they arrived forty-five minutes later, I was prepared to be their mother again. I felt the heat, but now it surrounded me as if it were outside my body. There was a part of me that stayed in the moment and another part that seemed to evaporate. The video image never stopped playing.

When the girls entered the cabin, I was able to be present for them. Two girlfriends who had been sharing the cabin with them came along. Both knew Pam well and were crying, too. My daughters fell into my arms, braced their bodies against mine, and together we shared our sorrow. But not a single tear fell from my eyes. It was as if I had turned to stone. I was in shock, but did not know it.

The girls begged me to leave with them on an early morning flight to Florida that left from Greensboro, nearly three hours away. They'd already made the travel arrangements, but the heat and paralysis in my body would not let me move. The thought of driving three more hours after the twenty-four hours Jim and I had already been on the road was unbearable. I told them that I needed to stay and take a later plane. They left reluctantly, and as they walked out the door looking back toward me, I knew once more that my life had changed forever.

The circumfused heat seemed to engulf me. I felt my flesh burning, as if being devoured by an invisible fire. Something was terribly wrong.

After much insistence, Jim drove me to Cannon Memorial Hospital, the closest place where I could receive medical attention. As I walked into the emergency room, a nurse recognized my emotional state and called the doctor immediately. It wasn't necessary to give the details. The doctor also recognized my condition after taking my blood pressure: 180/100. He confirmed my state of shock and offered me a sedative, which I refused. I felt it would impair my ability to think clearly. I knew I had to be up by five in the morning to catch an early flight, and the sedative might make the trip more difficult.

I felt as if I was in a nightmare and could not escape. I wanted to wake up but didn't want to accept what had happened. Reality was too painful. I kept asking myself, How could this happen? What could I have done to change the sequence of events that resulted in her suicide?

My mind raced with endless questions and self-flagellation. Why hadn't I made it my business to find an institution where she could get the care she needed? Why had I been so short with her when she needed reassurance and compassion the most? How had I let her fall through the cracks? How had she slipped through my fingers? Why had she jumped? Would I ever really know? Could I go on without knowing why my daughter had taken her own life? What had gone through her mind minutes before she plunged to her death? Why? Why? Why?

This was the week of my life I wanted to rewrite. This was the week I wanted to do over. This would be my angst until I learned to forgive myself and let go. But first I had to go through the grief.

2

THE DAY AFTER

July 3, 1998

The next morning my plane prepared for landing at the Fort Lauderdale airport. As it began its descent, a strange, gray, numinous mist clouded the familiar landscape. Fires were ravaging the Florida Everglades nearby, leaving the land charred and lifeless. It seemed so timely, a perfect backdrop of gloom for my daughter's funeral. As we exited the sliding doors onto the terminal's arrival pick-up area, the heat hammered us, a gentle reminder that it was indeed July—one of the hottest months of the year—and how quickly the forest fires had inflamed the already oppressive Florida heat.

I drove home with a man I hardly knew who had insisted that he accompany me. I was annoyed and embarrassed by his unwelcome presence. I tried to convince him that this was not his place, but I was too weak to argue. I felt lifeless.

I showered and rummaged through the hamper for a black suit that had been waiting to be sent to the cleaners upon my return. It was wrinkled from lying in a pile of other dirty clothes, but it was all I had that I felt appropriate to wear. I glanced in the mirror in horror. My face was not mine. I could not recognize myself. My eyes were swollen from all the crying. I wore a look of both shock and horror. I was shattered and still in a state of disbelief that I was going to attend my daughter's funeral. I felt like I had fallen into a surrealistic dream haunted by a reality I was not yet ready to accept.

People filled the funeral parlor. There were some my family and I knew and some we didn't—bad news travels fast. My ex-husband Paul had made all the arrangements before I had even learned of Pam's death. I was grateful not to have had the responsibility and thankful that my parents had not lived long enough to witness this.

Still in shock, I didn't know quite what to do, how to act, even how to feel. I fluctuated between disbelief and numbness between inconsolable grief and a strange sense of relief: it was finally over—those years of torment for her and for all of us—at last, a finale. One minute I felt aware of my physical presence, then the next I seemed to vanish as if trapped in an altered state.

I waited in the chapel's family quarters while the main chapel filled with a steady stream of the many people who had been a part of Pam's life, both directly and indirectly, recently and in the past. As I scanned the room, my eyes locked on to a small group of people wearing orthodox attire. The men wore long black coats, their heads donned with either the traditional skullcaps or large black hats. Most of them had long side curls dangling in front of their ears. The women wore hats that completely covered their hair. They wore no makeup, making every effort to disguise their sensuality and minimize their femininity, as is common in their tradition. I recognized them as members of the Chabad, a community of very religious Jews who had embraced Pam in her search for answers and hope just a few months before her death. They had tried to cultivate a relationship with her, hoping she could learn how to connect with God according to their beliefs and practices. I was surprised to see them there. They were strangers to me yet they seemed to know all about her, which left me feeling awkward in their presence.

I spotted Paul, whom I had married thirty-five years before and then divorced thirteen years later. Although it had been over twenty years since our divorce, it felt as if no time had passed at all. I was suddenly swept into a time warp; he felt like my husband yet again. Our eyes met for the first time since Pam had died. It was as if we were the only two people in the room. We moved toward each other, like two magnets drawn together. Our hearts had joined together once more, but this time it was through tragedy.

He opened his arms and embraced me, his left hand cradling my head against his chest, and we cried, sharing the grief that only parents can know. As he held me in his arms, his familiar fragrance of Aramis took me back to when and how it all began.

᙭

I had grown up like any average girl in America during the fifties, although Miami Beach was not your average town. It was more like living in a make-believe world, an indestructible bubble. Life was good. Times were easy. Alcohol and drug addiction were almost nonexistent in our culture. We drank wine only on the Jewish holidays. My parents stayed married in the traditional and expected "till death do us part" style. They weren't perfect but who is? Perhaps our family had some dysfunction; mild compared to what many consider unhealthy or abnormal family relationships today.

We were poor, but so was everyone else in our neighborhood. We weren't aware of class distinctions until we entered Beach High, the only high school in the city. There we learned about the haves and the have-nots. We didn't know if we fit in, but we managed to find our own way and grow up in spite of our social and economic differences. We had our own Mason Dixon line: Lincoln Road. Those who lived north of that line were considered wealthy and upper middle class, while those who lived south of it were low on the economic scale. Even though many egos were trampled and hearts broken, we grew up believing that Beach kids were special.

Blacks were called "colored," and they sat in the backs of the buses, without any obvious disdain. They had their own water fountains and bathrooms; and it never even occurred to us that this was racial discrimination. Apartheid was the norm for the time.

It was the 1950s, the last age of innocence. We skated every

Friday night in Flamingo Park, never giving a thought to muggings or rape. We ate dinner together at the dining room table with our families, saved our allowances, and followed the rules. We tried to model our lives after *Leave It to Beaver*, *Father Knows Best*, and the Nelson family from *The Adventures of Ozzie and Harriet*. Television during the fifties captured the family norms, social mores, values, and moralities of its time. Profanity- and violence-free wholesome entertainment and laughter filled the screen. *I Love Lucy* was our favorite comedy show. The music of our era helped define us. Rock 'n' roll blasted from the jukeboxes of every diner and soda shop, car radios, and phonographs. Bill Haley and the Comets had touched off a musical revolution with "Rock Around the Clock," and by the time Elvis appeared on *The Ed Sullivan Show*, the Victorian attitudes gasped its dying breath, and the sexual revolution shot out of the starting gate. Hula hoops, poodle skirts, and ponytails were in; bobby socks, crooners, and the jitterbug were out.

Most of us married young. Babies soon followed. Then things seemed to change. The social and sexual revolutions of the sixties invaded our innocence and distorted our values and ideals. We were no longer in the "age of innocence." Martin Luther King Jr. set us straight. By the time he was gone and the Kennedy brothers had been assassinated, we were grieving the loss of our innocence along with their deaths.

Nearly half of everyone I grew up with divorced within seven years of marriage. Most of the divorced women went back to school for degrees in social work, got real estate licenses, or became interior decorators. Some remarried; others never did. Most of us went to parties, football games, attended college, worked, and took care of our homes and children.

During the Cuban Missile Crisis, the thirteen days when the world almost blew up, I met the man who would become the father of my five children. As we were enjoying our first date eating apple strudel at The Rascal House in Sunny Isles, Florida, Bobby Kennedy struck the deal that saved the world.

It was October 1961. Paul was twenty-five years old, serving an internship in Miami with less than a year to complete his medical training. He was full of ambition and enough passion to capture the world. I had been divorced for three months from my first husband when I met him. Never having been consummated, my teenage marriage of two years had been annulled. I wrote it off as something that should never have been.

"I'm never getting married," Paul had protested from the get-go. But his words made little impact on me and within eight months we were married. We had walked down the aisle, innocent and unprepared for what was yet to come: a mixed bag of joy and shattered dreams.

My reverie crashed when Paul released me from his embrace and looked at me with eyes that spoke more than he could voice. He pressed his lips together and then released a heavy sigh. He dabbed his swollen and weeping eyes with an already wet handkerchief and turned, moving into the crowd. My heart ached for him as much as it did for me.

Tinted jet-black hair framed the thin olive, grief-stricken face of the woman who approached me in a wheelchair—Astrid, Paul's girlfriend. Just a few days before Pam died, Astrid had fallen and broken her leg. She was the last one to see Pam alive.

She wheeled herself over to me and looked directly into my eyes. Her Spanish accent and tremulous voice distorted her words. "I am so sorry," she said.

Empathy transcended the aloofness and intimidation she seemed to project during the fifteen years she and Paul had been together. I had always experienced a tacit discomfort with her during those years, but that disappeared in this one empathetic moment. On this day, she was nothing but genuine and compassionate. The mother in her consoled the mother in me. We connected.

"I wish I could have done something," she whispered.

Her pain mirrored mine. Her eyes were moist. I heard her, but nothing registered.

"Pam kissed me good-bye. That kiss should have been for you," she said, then, tears flowed.

I wondered what she meant, but I would ask her later. She clasped my hands in hers and pulled me down to her. She leaned forward and kissed my cheek. That was the first time she had ever touched me.

My eyes shifted toward my youngest son, Aaron, who quickly approached us. He wanted us to view Pam in the coffin and say good-bye to her, but it was more than I could bear. She had plunged to her death from fifteen stories onto concrete. I didn't want to see the damage to her body, making my last good-bye inconceivable. The children and I anguished over this decision. Aaron thought it wise to have closure. None of us wanted to remember her the way she died. Not yet twenty-five years old, Aaron took it upon himself to take the first look and assess whether we could handle the viewing. He returned wearing a relieved smile, then he lead us to her. Although terrified of what we might see, we accepted his encouragement and approached reluctantly, cautiously.

Barry, whom Pam had lived with at the Chabad community a few months earlier, kept vigil over her coffin all evening at the funeral home. He administered the ritual prayers for her as they prepared her body for the traditional Jewish cleansing and burial. It disturbed me that he took the liberty to exercise this vigil. I felt it was an intrusion, that this was not his place. Pam would not have been happy.

I was not sure she would have wanted him praying over her, but in retrospect, he was a blessing. He provided patience, understanding, and unyielding love. He had been a constant support throughout those perilous times and thought foremost of her welfare. The ritual he performed during the evening she lay in her coffin could have only come from the purest heart and mind.

I had to find a place to displace my anger and Barry had unwittingly become my scapegoat. It took time and distance for me to realize he and Pam possessed a bond that perhaps none of us understood. My knowledge of Judaism was so limited that I could not appreciate the spiritual connection they shared and the gifts he had bestowed upon her. I saw them through my eyes only, and my vision was distorted with my own map of reality. I needed to expand my belief system to understand Barry's genuine devotion and commitment to Pam. He had been her angel. Her illness drove her to him and then away from him. Throughout their separation, Barry stayed committed to her healing. He never abandoned her nor stopped loving her.

I walked toward the coffin. Pam lay in repose inside its tufted, white satin lining. Wrapped in a white shroud with a gossamer head covering that framed her exquisite and miraculously unmarred face, her head was tilted slightly to the right, and her eyes were closed. A halo of light surrounding her head radiated over her youthful and innocent face. Her appearance was like that of an angel. On her beautiful, serene face, I saw peace and tranquility for the first time in years. The tension she had worn for so long was gone. I looked at her for a long time. I wanted to remember this moment, this last good-bye. I was happy to see her at peace at last. I bent over her cold, covered body, kissed her gently, and said good-bye to my little girl who had come and gone like an angel.

Paul, our children, and I entered the main chapel, where we took our places on the front row. The room was filled to capacity. People stood against the walls. As I sat in the pew waiting for the service to begin, I thought about how difficult these last few years had been—perhaps the most difficult of my life. My mother had died in January 1993 and my father in April 1997. It's strange that when you lose both your parents, your mortality smacks you in the face and you realize so poignantly that you're the next generation. But you never expect that your child will go before you.

For me, a stampede of losses began with the loss of my father, who died suddenly of congestive heart failure just one month before his eighty-ninth birthday, only one month after he had walked down the aisle at Pam's wedding and two months prior to my eldest son Todd's marriage.

In June, one week after their wedding, Todd and his bride left for Ohio where he began his residency in obstetrics and gynecology; Aaron began a new job in Tallahassee; and my business partner, and friend, left South Florida to take a position in New Jersey. They all had departed within the same week. My sense of security on every level had been shaken and challenged. That same month, the landlord had informed me that I had to leave my office, giving me only two weeks to pack my things and find another one. I scrambled, frantically packing twenty-one years of collected materials, diplomas, certificates, charts, books, and memorabilia, all the while trying to find a new office.

Sam, my fourth husband, passed away unexpectedly of a precipitous, inoperable gangrene of the intestine in February of 1998. Then Chava, my closest friend, lost her interminable struggle with cancer in March. Paul's mother, my children's beloved grandmother, Dorothy, died in May, after several months of chronic illness. And now my daughter's funeral, less than two months from the day

we buried Dorothy. Five funerals and two weddings, all within a
year and a half.

To say that I was overwhelmed with the onslaught of unexpected
life changes was an understatement. I thought I would never adapt,
let alone recover. The losses I had endured had been too many,
too soon. I had not sufficiently grieved them before Pam's tragedy
shattered me.

I yearned for my father, who had been my mentor, my anchor,
my coach, and protagonist. Even though we were at war much of
the time, he was always "my daddy" in both our hearts. I spent the
last night of his life in his arms, huddled against his weakened body.
There was no place for me to sleep in the hospital, so I snuggled
up against him, my last chance to be his little girl once more.

I mourned my best friend, Chava. She suffered her fourth recur-
rence of cancer, which had been diagnosed fourteen years earlier,
before it finally took her vibrant life. We had been soul sisters.
While waiting for Pam's service to begin, I relived the nightmare
of Chava's illness.

In February 1997, with a heavy heart, I had boarded a flight
to Denver. I didn't know what to expect. Chava's daughter, Hilit,
had been with her mother days before, helping to prepare her for
the stem cell replacement that was to take place the following
day. Chava and Hilit needed my emotional and physical support.

After the treatment, I sat on the bathroom floor next to Chava, my arm around her most of the night and into the early morning hours as she repeatedly leaned over the commode retching and vomiting, a constant reminder of the poisonous remedy attacking her relentless cancer as well as any healthy remaining tissue.

"Joni, Joni," she cried. "It's so hard, but . . . I know if I keep fighting, I'll make it. Pray for me."

"Of course you will make it. I pray for you every day," I said, knowing she was closer to death than life. I was her friend, and any words of hope and encouragement I could offer were better than none. I felt like a fraud. I knew she could not go on much longer, but I was afraid to share my honest thoughts and feelings.

Hardly anyone survived this treatment, so she knew it was risky and the chances of success were slim, but she wanted this last-ditch attempt to save her life.

I made a pledge to myself that I would never do what she so courageously chose to do. She was brave and determined to fight this battle, choosing life at any cost. She fought against all the odds. She fought against her doctors. She had hope when there was no hope.

Her death had taken a long time, nearly a year after the procedure. In my view, it had been a year not worth living.

I was still mourning her.

I glanced around the chapel and saw so many faces, ones I hadn't seen in many years. Someone approached me, bending down to kiss my cheek.

"I'm so sorry," one said, wiping her tears. "I'm so sorry."

One by one people converged, like a receiving line in a wedding. Only today, there were no congratulations, no best wishes. Today there were only condolences and sympathy.

My body seemed to switch to autopilot as I mechanically shook hands and accepted hugs. My mind took me back to my other losses. I thought of Sam, my fourth husband, who had passed away six months earlier.

In 1989, Sam had bought a cabin in Banner Elk, North Carolina. After driving a few miles leisurely looking for property in the mountains, something we spoke about often but never found the time to do, we saw a small sign on the side of Highway 194 that said "cabin for sale."

As we drove onto a dirt road, we came upon a scene that took our breath away. I thought we had driven into a time of years gone by that reminded me of a Thomas Kinkade painting. There in the glen of an apple orchard surrounded by North Carolina pine trees, evergreens of several varieties, and rhododendron bushes, a cabin was nestled under some extended branches of an old apple tree. I expected to hear the refrains of Beethoven's Pastoral Symphony at any moment.

As our car approached the cabin, on our right we saw tall trees towering over two small ponds and on our left was a brook adjacent to another pond close to the cabin. Peonies stood tall in front of the porch. A large wagon wheel leaned against the front door. The door and windows were framed in red and green as if the house was to be used in a Gucci commercial; it was a sudden shift from one century to another. Sam stopped the car and we both stepped out in disbelief. It took two days to negotiate the purchase. I was excited when he finalized the purchase, even gleeful like a little girl who had won the grand prize at a carnival.

"I can't believe it's ours! It's the most enchanting place in the universe!" I squealed.

We were so happy making the renovations it needed to accommodate us. We went there every summer and often in the fall. I loved it most in fall when the leaves changed into brilliant shades of reds, golds, and yellows, as if God had used the mountains as a palette, choosing the colors carefully to paint each leaf a different color from the other. It had only God's signature.

It was in our one hundred-fifty-year-old, hand-hewn rustic cabin that we held our annual Thanksgiving dinner. The kids and I would drive the winding mountain roads, singing "Over the River and Through the Woods." We were cramped in such a tiny space, but it didn't stop us from eating our way into oblivion, playing charades, singing holiday songs, and just hanging out. The girls helped me prepare the meals and the boys made the fire and set the table. Laughter and chatter filled the little cabin.

It was a time of renewal when we reestablished our bonds, settled our differences, and reaffirmed our love for one another. When we parted, it was with the promise to return again the following year.

Although Pamela and Sam did not have the same fondness for each other as did the other children, the time together at the cabin resolved their conflicts and brought them closer.

Sam planted a maple tree in the summer of '91. It was only twelve inches high, a cutting from our neighbor's tree. It grew a little taller and thicker as each season came and went. Every June we took a photo of Sam and his beloved maple tree.

Our divorce changed everything. The cabin was no longer mine. It saddened me once more to think those years were gone.

Sam's unexpected death shocked and dismayed me. More a father figure than a husband, he had showered his strength and love upon me with unyielding devotion. He'd provided the nurturing I was starving for, but the twenty-year age span created irreconcilable differences in spite of his abundant generosity and kindness. I mourned the life we couldn't have and the time we did have.

Even before all these losses occurred, I had decided to take a sabbatical in July and August, something I had never done in the history of my professional life. I had wanted to go back to North Carolina. When I scheduled my time off, I had no way of knowing that my best friend, mother-in-law, ex-husband, father, and daughter were all going to die. Some part of me, some primordial, archetypal energy that resides deep within my soul, had driven me to take at sabbatical for these two months

I shifted back to the present, sitting in the front pew of the funeral chapel, next to the man who had fathered our deceased daughter, our firstborn child. His left hand held my right. My eyelids were swollen and puffy from an unflagging stream of tears and sleep deprivation. I glanced at my four remaining children seated to my left, my heart heavy. Never had I seen them so sad. The obvious absence of Pam, who lay in the coffin resting on the stage in front of us, felt surrealistic. We were locked together in our grief, joined by thoughts, feelings, and shock.

The rabbi, wearing the traditional black robe and yarmulke (the skullcap donned to honor God), stepped up to the pulpit. The ark that housed the sacred Torah was closed behind him. His dark beard flecked with gray seemed to remain the same over the passing years, as did his unflattering, ill-fitting toupee. He was an honest man, and the toupee seemed silly and incongruous to his authenticity.

The rabbi and I were life-long friends. He officiated at the baby naming when Pam was just two months old, at her Bat Mitzvah, and at her wedding. He had visited with Pam only one week earlier. She had been separated from her husband, Kevin, for a few months. In her effort to try to determine the legitimacy of her "get," the Jewish divorce document, Pam, accompanied by her youngest sister, Erika, went to the rabbi's home in hopes of obtaining some reassurance and perhaps some blessings. He called me just after their visit, worried that she was out of touch with reality and wondering if I knew how bad she was. I assured him that I was aware of how deteriorated she had become and how frustrated I was with not finding an appropriate treatment facility. Kind and supportive, he knew from his own experience how draining a mental illness could be on the family. He felt my pain. His ex-wife had been in treatment most of her adult life with schizophrenia and had spent most of her adult years in a mental institution.

As he leaned over the lectern and looked at us, I considered how quickly time had passed as I recalled him blessing Pam at her Hebrew naming ceremony in December 1963.

Although her given name was Pamela, her father and I had given her the Hebrew name Pinina, meaning "pearl," after my paternal grandfather, Philip. The rabbi had smiled at her as if she were one of his own. He'd lifted her, proudly presenting her to her Maker as well as the entire congregation. He'd asked God to bless her and give her long life. He'd prayed for a future husband and many children.

My thoughts fast-forwarded to her Bat Mitzvah. Not quite thirteen years old, Pam and the rabbi had stood by the pulpit. She'd looked like an angel in her long white robe with her golden hair falling below her shoulders. He'd stretched out his arms over her head as he blessed her. When finished, he smiled and praised her for her *gitte neshuma*, Hebrew for "good soul," and acknowledged her intellect, her beauty, and her devotion to her family and God. He'd blessed her once again for a long, rich, and fruitful life.

My thoughts jumped to the last time he had officiated at a milestone for her: her wedding day, only a little over a year ago. She had been so radiant in her wedding dress. Albeit nervous and anxious, she had so wanted to fulfill this lifelong dream.

I will never forget how beautiful she had looked on the day she'd dreamed about for so many years. She stood alongside Kevin under the chupa (wedding altar) with the rabbi. Gazing into the eyes of her groom, she'd recited her original nuptials, her eyes welling up with tears. To the audience, her tears were of joy, but I knew the truth—they were tears of sorrow. Regardless, her words were as exquisite as her presence. Kevin's response paled against hers. After taking their vows, the rabbi had blessed them, wishing them a long and happy marriage filled with the laughter and joy of children (none of which happened; another false prophecy like at her naming ceremony and Bat Mitzvah).

I looked up at the rabbi. He caught my eye. I could see that he resonated with my despair. We may have even been remembering the same memories, but I continued to drift into the past. Memories of her wedding day took me back to the time she had met Kevin. The thoughts were disturbing, for they reminded me of how ill she was and how unaware we were.

Pam's greatest desire had been to marry and have children. But every relationship had ended in disappointment. Her mood swings and eccentric behaviors caused by her undiagnosed bipolar disorder undermined the course and outcome of each relationship. Her patterns and erratic responses drove her partners away, leaving her increasingly depressed and plunging her deeper into her pathology.

Kevin and Pam had met at a picnic for Jewish singles. He had appeared oblivious to her symptoms. His own inadequacies and undiagnosed spectrum disorder kept him aloof and unaware. Her beauty, talent, intelligence, and engaging personality disguised her illness enough to allow him to find her fascinating rather than mentally ill. He tolerated what previous boyfriends had not.

Returning home from the picnic, she seemed excited about meeting Kevin. But then her impression of him changed as she described to me how, to her, he somewhat resembled a vampire. She said that he frightened her, but she assumed her hallucinations were a probable cause for this delusion. This revelation, the fact that she recognized that it was a hallucination, of course stunned us.

Meeting Kevin and her vampire hallucinations triggered an episode that resulted in her hospitalization just a few days later. Kevin's lack of awareness and interest in Pam's mental state startled me and our family. He visited her at the hospital all day, each and every day requesting that we bring him food from The Epicure Market, but he showed no sensitivity to cost or propriety. His attitude was that of entitlement because he was her self-proclaimed boyfriend. During her stay in the hospital, Pam changed her mind about him and saw him as the "most wonderful man in the world; a saint." She protected him to a fault.

During their year of courtship, Pam desperately tried to convince herself and everyone else that Kevin was her soul mate, her *beshert* ("the man chosen for her by God"). She seemed to be out of control quite often, precipitating arguments that manifested aggressive behaviors. Kevin seemed to fuel her fire, perhaps because he lived with her. I don't think she was much different with me; however, sometimes, when she was with me, she could step out of the illness and separate herself from it.

They married in March 1997, for all the wrong reasons. As their marriage progressed, Kevin withdrew more and more. Unable to reconnect with Pam, he went MIA into his own world, ignoring her and withdrawing from the relationship. This infuriated Pam. She demanded his presence and interaction, but Kevin was incapable of being in any relationship, let alone one with her. Her demands and criticisms pushed him farther away, until he disappeared emotionally. This dynamic produced a vicious cycle of arguments where she would lash out like a tyrant, and he would go into silent violence. It was a polluted relational space with toxic energy to which they grew accustomed to living in.

Kevin was a man without a sense of self. He was not in touch with his feelings, unable to express himself yet hopelessly smitten with Pam. He was thirty-seven years old and she was his first girlfriend. She'd had dozens of boyfriends, numerous one-night stands and casual affairs, three serious relationships, and one previous engagement. Her experience in romance and sex was light years ahead of his. Her knowledge of communication skills and intimacy with herself and others made him seem like he was from another planet. The disparity was enormous; yet, they shared a common interest. They both were desperate to be married. She felt like time and men were passing her by. Most of her girlfriends had been married and either had children or were expecting. To her, getting married was more important than whom she was marrying. She sold out for the sake of being wed.

It was terrifying to stand by and watch her compromise values she had held true to her heart. I knew it. Her father knew it. Her siblings and friends knew it. We were powerless to stop this travesty and equally sorrowful.

But even with all the inner turmoil, dressed in her full length, tulle, wedding gown, Pam had looked like a princess. Her golden brown hair had been pulled back tight in a bun at the nape of her neck, with tiny braids woven into the form of a flower. Her sister Monica, an expert hair designer, created an elegant coif to host the six-foot veil that trailed behind her. The silver-beaded tiara that crowned her head adorned her with the grace and dignity of royalty. She needed little makeup, but with the proper shading and color on her lips, cheeks, and eyes, she was a work of art.

The wedding party waited outside in the corridor until we were called to begin walking down the aisle. Pam trembled as each bridesmaid was motioned forward. She was a nervous wreck. Her body spoke to me with its own language, stronger than any words might convey. Clearly, she knew she was making a mistake. The tears running down her cheeks, smudging her makeup and smearing her mascara, were not a bride's tears of joy. Albeit she was in touch with her intuition and deep feelings, she was equally capable of rationalizing and denying them. With a heavy heart, I knew unequivocally what was in hers.

"Pami, dear, you don't have to go through with this. We can call it off right now."

She looked at me so perplexed, apparently half relieved that I was giving her a way out, and half fearful that the wedding might be aborted.

"Honestly, sweetheart, I can take care of it right now. All you have to do is give me the okay."

Her father, standing beside us, was stunned, yet in agreement. "Better now than later," he said. I felt I could read his mind and perceived him saying to himself, *This can't be happening.*

The harpist and flutist began playing Pachelbel's Canon as we watched each of the twelve bridesmaids walk out the corridor door onto the red carpet.

"I can't. Not now. It's too late!" she cried.

"No! It's not too late. It's okay to change your mind. You will not be the first bride to do it nor the last," I said, hoping she would give me permission to stop the wedding.

"What would you say to the people? The rabbi and cantor are already under the chupa. It would be too embarrassing. I can't do it. I just can't!"

"Pam, if you give me permission, your father and I would simply walk down the aisle to the chupa, and I would take the microphone, face our guests, and announce that I have good news and bad news. The bad news is that the marriage is off. The good news is that we're having a party!"

It didn't work. The music changed to "Here Comes the Bride." Her father and I put both our arms inside hers and together, we walked her down the aisle.

In spite of her ambivalence and fear, in spite of her smudged makeup from weeping and wiping her tears away, she had been the most beautiful bride I had ever seen.

My attention returned to the present, to our family, friends, and colleagues gathered together under the same roof to say good-bye to Pam, to mourn her death, and to pray. Rabbi Brunswick, our teacher, leader, and old friend, although small in stature was huge in spirit, a living legend of our faith. Tears ran down his wrinkled cheeks. He reached for a handkerchief inside his robe and blew his nose. Arching his brows and then screwing up his eyes, he looked at us, this time with only the face of tragedy. He began his eulogy.

I don't remember much of what he said. What will remain with me always and what was most meaningful were these words:

"Ask yourselves if you would rather not have had Pam at all, knowing her destiny, or if knowing her for the thirty-four years of her life were better than not having her at all."

His black robe and yarmulke made him appear holy and gave me comfort, but the look of mercy and anguish upon his face made him appear human, giving me a sense of connection and empathy that I so desperately needed. When he finished, he asked us if we wanted to say something. We had each prepared something the night before. I had tried to scratch a few words down while on the plane. How do you write a eulogy for a daughter? How do her siblings write one for their sister? What can be said in a few words that could describe what she meant to each of us?

A hand went up in the crowd. He nodded for her to come forward. Lisa, Pam's best friend from childhood, had flown in on the red-eye from Colorado. Everyone followed her with their eyes as she approached the podium. Lisa spoke softly, but with great strength. She spoke of her friendship with Pam, the years they had shared, and the lives they could no longer have together. She said she would mourn the children Pam would never have. She highlighted experiences from their past with passion, laughter, and sorrow. She had been a constant support to Pam as her illness progressed. A clinical psychologist, Lisa had offered her unyielding counsel and loving support.

Our guests began to emote. Their hearts ached for our loss and what could have easily been theirs. The hand of fate writes its own script. There was not a dry eye among us. The honor and praise she so graciously and eloquently delivered touched us all.

Then Cathy solemnly walked to the pulpit. She too had taken the red-eye, hers from LA, arriving just in time for the funeral. Cathy's blonde curly hair was coiffed close to her exquisite face, and her voice sounded like a song as she took the microphone and spoke. Her refrains of love and friendship were heartwarming and heartbreaking. She cherished Pam. She celebrated her life and mourned her death. Pam and Cathy had met in their freshman year of college at the University of Missouri. Cathy, a gentle young woman, had supported Pam through her long illness, encouraging her to have faith and to trust in God and herself. She prayed for her ritually every night during the years Pam suffered.

Both eulogies were expressions of devotion and healing to our hearts. One by one, my children took the microphone, each having their own story.

Monica's message was about sisterhood and how Pam had been there when she was born. Monica had never known life without her older sister. She spoke of the early bonding and how Pam had been her role model through the years. She shared her pride and fondest of memories. She recalled personal anecdotes about their history, some funny and some sad. She had been the last to provide a home for Pam and was the last of her siblings to learn of her death.

"This never should have happened," she cried. "Pam loved life."

Once again my mind regressed to late in the evening of June 29, 1965. I had been riding in the passenger seat of my girlfriend's car as we hurried toward Mount Sinai Hospital. Oh, how I remembered the pain. My labor had begun about 7:00 PM, shortly after I had put away the dinner dishes and tucked Pam into bed. I was about two weeks overdue and had gone to the hospital two weeks prior only to be sent home with false labor. This time, it was for real. The pains were coming five minutes apart, and it felt like I was going to rip apart. I contained the screams, howling in my innermost being. I writhed, put my head down, and squeezed my legs together. I prayed and cursed the whole way.

"Just go fast, Phyllis. I don't know if I am going to make it."

"You'll make it. Just breathe. I'll get you there. Just breathe."

My breathing sounded like a wounded animal hoping to be put out of its misery.

"Oh, God, Phyl, why do we have to go through this shit? Where the fuck is Paul? Why is he never here when I need him?"

Paul had been invited to a stag party, which meant a craps table in someone's Florida room with a dozen or so frenzied men shooting dice across a table while shouting rhetoric and words familiar to most gamblers. I had called him as soon as the pains were closer together, but he casually assured me it was just false labor again.

"How can you be so sure? I am two weeks late. Maybe you had better come home," I pleaded.

"No. I don't need to come home. Just relax, and you'll be fine. I'll check you when I get home."

Fuck this. I called my girlfriend Phyllis, and she was there in ten minutes, walking me to the car, and trying her best to keep both of us calm. Here I was, rushing down I-95 about to have my second baby and my husband was shooting craps!

Monica was born before Paul had made it to the hospital. Disappointed that we'd had another girl, all he could say was how much she looked like Buddy Hackett.

My memories shot forward to when Monica was fourteen. I had always thought of Monica as my love child. She was the one who carried my feelings, who tried to mend my pain, who wrote loving notes when I came home from work and school, trying to soothe my temperament. She was the peacemaker, the caregiver, and a gentle spirit who didn't seem to have a mean bone in her body . . . until she turned fourteen. Perhaps it was the age or all the men who by now had downloaded my life like files in a computer. She had accepted Dennis, the man I married after Paul and I were divorced; but accepting Jerry, the five-year-long live-in boyfriend who followed Dennis, proved difficult for her. He had come on the heels of Dennis's leaving the house. No grass ever grew under my feet, I reflected with self-contempt.

Monica had built up resentment and rage, feeling that Jerry had taken me from her. She began acting out. As if a wall had gone up, we separated both physically and emotionally. All the things I thought she would never be capable of doing, she did. She lied, sneaked around, withdrew from me, broke all the rules, and was chronically truant from school.

Monica was totally out of control and had run away at least three times. After she had returned the last time, I stood in my foyer, crying, pleading, and screaming. "You are going to your father whether you like it or not! Get your things and get ready. Jerry is taking you to the airport, and your father will be waiting there for you."

She spewed, cried, and challenged all of us with a vengeance I never knew she possessed. As she saw it, no one would make her go to Missouri. No one could tell her what to do.

"I'm not going! I don't have to listen to him. He's not my father." A familiar refrain I had heard countless times before.

"You'd better put your pants on, young lady, or you are going to be flying on that plane in your flip-flops and T-shirt!" Jerry shouted.

"I'm not going!"

My brother, Mickey, was there for moral support. He tried hard to reason with her and thought that the tenor of their relationship would lend understanding and capitulation. But she would not budge. Monica was determined to have her way.

In a matter of moments, wearing flip-flops, and a T-shirt, she was scurried out of the house and physically coerced into the passenger seat of Jerry's car, holding a hairbrush in her right hand. And that's exactly how Jerry had put her on the plane. He gave fair warning to both the pilot and airline attendant, alerting them that she was a runaway and that her father would be waiting for her when they arrived.

In less than forty-eight hours, she was back in Miami before Paul had even realized that she was gone. She had purchased a bus ticket bought with money her girlfriend had stolen then sent to her. When she returned, she surreptitiously fled to her girlfriend's apartment without any desire to return home to me. This time I did not to try to bring her home. It would be futile, just another reason for her to run away again. We had tried it so many times before. Instead, I played the string out. Three weeks elapsed; I heard nothing. I don't think I slept more than ten hours that whole time in those three weeks. I worried and feared that something terrible might occur. I thought of drugs, rape, and every other imaginable atrocity that might happen . . . even murder. I prayed, ruminated horror stories, anguished over every potential possibility, and hoped she would feel homesick, lonely, remorseful, and desperate to return home.

I admit to using some healthy maternal manipulation and guilt, believing that I was entitled to these tactics as long as the outcome was in her best interest. I had instilled the right values, even if she was doing the wrong things. I gathered up childhood photos, memorabilia, and any items that would trigger positive feelings and a yearning to return home. I put together a scrapbook filled with personal sentiments and photos, and I made sure she received it.

It didn't take long. She came home ever so humble, apologetic, and with a willingness to make up for all she had done. She has never stopped. Somehow, with the grace of God, the help of all my maternal archetypes, the passing of time, and holding tenaciously to my beliefs, I had my daughter back once more.

I was startled back to the present when my son Todd walked up to the podium. His grief was visible in his shaking and inability to complete a sentence without breaking up. Erika walked up and stood alongside him for moral and physical support.

"Pam, my beautiful sister . . ." He began to weep. His body trembled. He lost his composure and, for a moment, his voice. Erika gently urged him to go on, assuring him that he was doing fine.

"May your spirit and soul rest in peace." The sobbing continued.

Erika put her arm on his right shoulder, stood very close, and spoke softly in his ear but loud enough for me to hear. "You can do this! Pam needs to hear your voice. Go on."

He spoke with such a heavy heart that I believe he carried the tears of God with him.

"Pam," he whispered while tears streamed down his tormented face, "you were the firstborn child, the first daughter, the apple of Grandpa's eye. You were our leader. I have never been a part of this world without you."

The words came from his soul. His body riveted with a grief he had never experienced. The shock of losing his sister overcame his stoic nature. He closed his eyes. No doubt he feared that if he kept them open, he would see the truth, for the coffin lay only a few feet away.

"We were five, and now we are four. You were the engine and Aaron the caboose; the two bookends. The point of the arrow aimed high." He opened his eyes only to close them again as tears rolled down his cheeks. He struggled to breathe as his body trembled.

"Some things I will always remember are when we were kids and all five of us took baths together in Mom's big bathtub. You would always pull my hair, and I would mess up your eyebrows. I will always remember that funny language you made up with names like Inky and Fredala. Your death, this funeral, that coffin all seem like a bad dream, a nightmare, and I just want to wake up.

"We had so many good times: dancing and singing just being together, one for all and all for one. Our lives became so complicated. If only you could come back to us. No words can describe what I am feeling. You are my big sister. You taught me how to drive. I followed your guidance through school. You helped me with my homework. You were the one who was always great with spelling and writing.

"We were 'the fabulous five.' No more. We will celebrate the thirty-four years we had with you. We will cherish those memories deeply and forever. As the sun sets in the west and the moon rises in the east, memories of you run through my mind. The sky appears tranquil like your spirit. The ocean is calm like your soul. The sky is radiant, as you are. You are there smiling down on us. I feel your presence. You will always be with us."

He raised his right arm, as if in salute. "Carpe diem, Pami. Seize the day!"

He regained his composure and spoke the words he had written and felt the day and night before. His sister had entered his spirit, and he did indeed feel her presence.

⁀

My thoughts slipped back to sometime in September 1997, a few months after Todd had married.

I had been in Athens, Ohio, visiting him and his wife during his internship. Under a lot of pressure and feeling uneasy, he had shared his lack of confidence and fear of not being good enough. He lamented that the program was so difficult and his attending physician impossible to please. He had been confronted, berated, scolded, and demeaned more often than his gentle soul could withstand.

"What if I don't make it, Mom? What if they don't think I'm good enough?"

I felt his fear, acknowledged it, and offered support and encouragement, but it never seemed to be enough. I knew how difficult this year would be for him. His plight toward medicine had always been a conflict in me. I feared that he had chosen the wrong path for his career. The sciences were his worst high school subjects. He made Cs and Ds in biology, physiology, anatomy, chemistry, and physics. He made As and Bs in literature, composition, political science, and history. It seemed he had chosen the path of most resistance, feeling compelled to live out the life of his father and grandfather's choice. There were too many constraints, so much to make the task more difficult than it had to be. The goal in life is to become what one is intended to be, not to live out someone else's unfulfilled ambitions. With the best of intentions, my father and perhaps Todd's father drilled into him their wishes and desires before Todd had a chance to realize his own. He defended them and his choice with so much conviction that it sounded like Gertrude from Hamlet, "The lady doth protest too much." Nevertheless, he plodded through those tormented years of medical school, internship, and residency with such fortitude and determination that he seemed to close the doors to any disruption or interference. His unrelenting will controlled his mind.

"I'm worried about Pami. Perhaps you should call her. I think she would love hearing from you," I said, hoping he would not feel manipulated, something I unintentionally provoked with all my children. Perhaps this trait was inherent in motherhood.

"Okay, Mom. I will. What's the problem?"

I had shared her problem with him many times. It was always the same nonchalant response. "I will" or "What's the problem?" or "She seems fine." His preoccupation with his internship, new marriage, too-dependent and complaining wife, and his compulsion to work harder and longer than anyone else kept him from hearing my message.

How could he be aware of her illness? He was making his own life, finding himself, settling into marriage, and attaining his personal goals. Pam's illness was a million miles away. Even if he did speak with her, he never heard or understood the depth and implications of her illness. It eluded so many others, even Pam's doctors. How could he be expected to understand the nature of her illness?

I recalled when Todd was only sixteen, he was with his father in Missouri, at the Lake of the Ozarks, to visit his father's girlfriend. It was then and there that the arrow of first love had pierced his young vulnerable heart. He fell in love with Laura. His love for her grew stronger each year. It sustained him through his adolescence and college. Yet it was a love not meant to last.

When Todd was living with his father in North Miami Beach, Todd convinced Laura to move in with them. Eventually, Todd asked her to marry him.

Laura left Todd the morning after he had given her an engagement ring. He awakened to a note and the ring. His heart must have stopped that day as the arrow that had been stuck there since puberty tried to withdraw. He called me. I was in the middle of a therapy session at my office. I excused myself and walked into the waiting room with the phone in my hand; I thought I heard his heart break.

He whimpered, hardly able to complete a sentence. "Mom, can you come get me?"

"Where are you?"

"I'm at school. Can you come?"

"Yes, of course I'll come. Stay there. I will be there in half an hour."

I excused myself from my client, grabbed my handbag and keys, and fled out of my office. I found my son leaning against a wall at the entrance of the medical school, his head buried in the curve of his right arm. His face was flushed from trying to hold back his tears. He shuffled down the stairs to the car.

"What happened? What's wrong?"

He couldn't speak. The words were there, but he could not mouth them.

"Tell me, Todd. What's wrong?" I pleaded.

"Laura left me. My Laura left me. I can't make it without her," he cried.

We drove to a local Chinese restaurant nearby the school. He hardly touched his lunch. His eyes remained moist and red throughout the meal.

"Look, Todd. I don't know why things happen the way they do. I don't have the answers to the questions. I only know that things happen for a reason. You must trust that there is a reason."

I paid the check and then drove toward the neighborhood we once lived in before he was born.

"Where are we going, Mom?"

"I am going to take you to the house you lived in when you were born. You were five when we moved. Do you remember the house?"

"No, well, maybe just a little. But why?"

"I want to show you something."

"What do you want to show me?"

"Wait. I'll explain."

I drove a short distance, as the community was not far from the restaurant. I turned down the street that we had once lived on and stopped in front of the house that had once been ours.

"Here it is." I said.

He looked quizzically at both the house and me. "And so? What about it?"

"It's not the house, Todd. It's what happened here that changed the course of your destiny."

"I don't know what you're talking about."

"Dr. Jackson used to live across the street." I pointed at their old house. "Dr. Kaufman lived four houses down the street. Dr. Zedeck on the corner, and two houses from him, Dr. Feldman." I pointed to each house as I identified their previous occupants.

"So what does all this have to do with Laura?"

I looked at my son, who, in this moment, felt like the only child in my life. He was searching for answers, for reasons, none that I could give him. Yet, I could give him hope. I could give him the truth.

"I never told you this, Todd. I never wanted you to carry this burden with you. But now is the appropriate time to disclose the facts about your birth."

"What happened? What are you talking about, Mom?"

"Monica was born in June 1965. By January 1966 I had not yet had a period. I went to see Dr. Feldman, the man who lived in that home." I pointed to the familiar house across from ours. "He told me I was pregnant. He was an anesthesiologist, not an obstetrician; but for reasons I still don't understand, the doctors' wives in our neighborhood went to him during their pregnancies. He delivered Pam."

"What does this have to do with anything?" His impatience was growing.

"I'm getting to it. Dr. Feldman diagnosed me as pregnant, requesting that I return in three weeks. I was astonished. I wondered how I could be pregnant again. I had just had a baby six months earlier. I was on birth control pills to try to induce my period while at the same time preventing another pregnancy. He took a pregnancy test, which at that time was called a rabbit test. If the rabbit died, then it was positive. Well, the rabbit died, and ostensibly, I was pregnant."

"Mom, I'm confused. I still don't understand all this."

"Just wait. I'll explain. Evidently Dr. Feldman did not realize that my uterus was still enlarged from Monica's birth and misinterpreted the enlargement as a uterus that was expanding due to a pregnancy; therefore, the diagnosis of pregnancy. I complained from January to June that I didn't feel pregnant. He consistently reassured me that I was. Finally, in mid-June I went for my monthly appointment, continuing to lament that I didn't feel pregnant. After all, I had already had two babies, so I knew what it felt like to be pregnant. He finally capitulated and examined me internally, where he discovered, to his dismay, that I was correct. He determined that the fetus was dead, explaining why it had not grown since his original exam at six weeks."

Todd stared at me curiously.

"I asked him what could be done. He said he could do a therapeutic abortion if I could obtain three signatures from two other physicians, plus his own, stating that the pregnancy had not progressed beyond six weeks because the fetus had died.

"I went to the other physicians that week, obtained the necessary papers, and was scheduled for this procedure in a few days. I remember it so well.

"It had been a Friday. I had handed the papers to Dr. Feldman. He made the necessary arrangements and said he would see me in a few days. Although apprehensive, I was relieved that I didn't have to carry around a dead fetus. Two days passed. It was Sunday morning and your father called me from his hospital rounds."

"Are you sitting down?" he asked.

"Yes, why?" It always made me nervous when Daddy began a question like that.

"Dr. Feldman died this morning."

"What?" Dismay filled me. I was shocked and unable to speak.

"Daddy had told me that Dr. Feldman, who was only thirty-nine years old, had been playing basketball with his kids at his home, collapsed on the court, and died of a massive heart attack. I was stunned."

I glanced at Todd, who appeared stunned as well.

"What does all this mean, Mom?"

"Well, instead of having my termination on Tuesday, I attended his funeral. There I was, in the back of the chapel, wearing a maternity outfit, thinking I was in my fifth month carrying a dead fetus. I was tearful, confused, and mourning for this young physician who was supposed to do a procedure that very day. Everything seemed so wrong. Why did this happen, I kept asking myself.

"I made an appointment to see the same obstetrician who had delivered Monica a year before. He examined me and told me to return again in three weeks. He was unable to determine if the fetus was dead, as he had never examined me to begin with and had no frame of reference to make a diagnosis. He needed more time. I returned three weeks later only to learn that I was about nine weeks pregnant. Strange as it may seem, Dr. Feldman had to die so you could be born."

Todd looked at me in disbelief, similar to the disbelief I felt when I learned that I was not pregnant in January, just misdiagnosed. Months later, I became pregnant due to my stopping the

birth control pills I had been on because I believed I was already pregnant.

"Look, Todd, I told you I don't have all the answers, but I do know this. If Dr. Feldman hadn't died, you and I would not be having this conversation now. And furthermore, Dr. Feldman had a birthmark, a patch of white hair above his brow. When you were born, you had the same white patch in the identical spot."

Todd sighed deeply, wiping his eyes as tears spilled down his cheeks. "I guess things do happen for a reason. I suppose one day I might understand why Laura left."

As I refocused my attention to the platform, Erika walked up to the podium and took the microphone from her brother. She spoke softly, reminding everyone how she too had held Pam in the highest regard and esteem. She declared that most of her success had been because Pam had been her mentor and coach. Pam had been her surrogate mother. She had been there when I was not. It had been Pam who tucked them into bed and read them a story. It had been Pam who encouraged them to sleep together, huddled in one bed to engender the safety and security they had missed in my absence.

Pam had given Erika confidence when she thought there was none. Pam had found the path when Erika felt lost. It had been Pam who had told her that nothing was impossible. Erika spoke of Pam as her guardian angel, then and forever.

"Pam's guidance and love will stay with me always. Even in her absence, her words will remain. When I am scared, I will recall her voice. When I am lonely, I will see her sweet face. When I feel lost, she will show me the way. Pam was my soul sister. Pam is in me." She tapped her heart. "Her broken body may be in that coffin," she pointed to the coffin that lay unopened on the dais, "but her soul and spirit are shared with mine."

Erika had been three years old when I had taken Monica to her organ lesson. I had left the children at home in the care of a young au pair from Ecuador. At the close of Monica's lesson, I had felt edgy. I had sensed an urgency to return home quickly.

Monica wanted pizza. I tried to dissuade her, hoping to feed her when we arrived home. She won out, even as my sense of urgency increased. While waiting for the pizza, I used the pay phone at the back of the pizza parlor to call home. As I dialed, my heart rate raced, my blood pressure seemed to rise, and my agitation increased.

Pam answered the phone. "Hello. Mommy? Mommy? Come home. Please come home. Erika had an accident and they took her to the hospital!"

A massive credenza with a marble and bronze candelabra had fallen on Erika's head as she tried to pull herself up. It fractured her skull and a portion of the frontal lobe of her brain had been exposed. It was Pam, then eight, who had run to the neighbors for help. They had called an ambulance and Erika had been rushed to the emergency room where a plastic surgeon had been called in to sew up the wound. By the time I had arrived at the hospital, the procedure was in process. I hurried into the recovery room. Standing by my little girl's bed, I stared down at this helpless child, her big hazel eyes seeming to communicate, "Mommy, help me," but no words came out, only my tears. She had sixty-seven stitches. A scar still remains as a reminder of that day.

Pami had taken responsibility to rescue her sister. The au pair had not only been hysterical but also totally helpless.

When Erika was sixteen, we lived in a three-bedroom apartment in North Miami Beach. Pam had been away at college and Monica was living on her own, leaving the three youngest children at home. I had been overwhelmed with working, managing motherhood and career, earning a living, and attending to the needs of three teenagers. Paul was living in Missouri. I had been torn as to which child needed me more, rendering me unable to give the proper attention to any of them.

Erika wanted to leave. Her best friend, my worst foe, lived in Chicago. Erika pleaded with me to let her go to Lisa's. She and Lisa had been childhood friends. I harbored anger and resentment undeservingly toward Lisa, believing she represented everything I didn't want Erika to become. She had been my nemesis, perhaps because she reflected all the things in my life that I disliked. Their friendship had more power than the relationship between Erika and me. I finally relented.

The experience was far better than I had hoped. Erika had a great time in the suburbs of Chicago. She met new friends who enjoyed and appreciated her. She did well in school, and Lisa's mother welcomed and made her feel part of the family. Erika found in Chicago what she was lacking here, including a boyfriend who had been her first lover.

Then it seemed that whatever good had come of that experience was about to be destroyed by disaster. Her boyfriend committed suicide by swallowing a gallon of antifreeze. Erika crumbled. She returned home, shaken with despair, shock, and severe depression. I was working as a clinical social worker, healing the wounded souls of others, yet was unable to help my own child.

A year earlier I had made my first mission to Israel. My experience had been so powerful and insightful, that I thought perhaps a trip to Israel might be just what she needed to get her out of that environment and distract her from her pain and loss. During their junior years in high school, both Pam and Todd had attended a six-week program called High School in Israel, which focused on the study of Western civilization. Both children revered the experience as one of the best in their lives. Intuitively, I had felt Erika should go, that it was the best course of action to take. She returned six weeks later, restored with wonderful memories that still live on.

I jerked back to the present when the youngest of my children, Aaron, came to the podium. At twenty-six years old, he appeared larger than life. His large-framed body seemed to loom across the lectern. He faced the overflowing crowd and stood silent for a moment. Then placing the microphone in its carriage and gripping the sides of the lectern, he leaned forward and spoke. His voice was strong, his words deliberate. He used no notes and repeated his brother's reference to Pam as the engine and himself as the caboose, identifying his siblings and himself as "the fabulous five."

"Now there are four," he said with strength and a strange sense of rejoicing. He put his fist in the air as he spoke with terse conviction.

"There will always be five. But, Monica," he said, looking directly at her, "you will be the engine now. I will still be the caboose. We can still move forward. We can do this for Pam. She would want us to continue on with her spirit, her wisdom, and her love. She prepared us for our journey, and even without her physical presence, she will continue to guide us. We will hear her voice in our hearts. She laid the foundation for us. We owe it to her to live our lives as she would have wanted us to. We are, and always will be, joined by our sister's soul. Pam was our pathfinder. She showed us the way. This is how we will honor her. We will revere her memory by becoming the people we were intended to become. Pam, our beloved sister, our devoted friend, our sibling soul mate, may your soul rest in peace."

Aaron spoke with the understanding and wisdom of a man twice his age. He seemed to possess a knowing, wise old soul. Every word he spoke sounded as if a spirit was channeling him far beyond his time.

When I discovered that I was pregnant with my fifth child, I had been in an experimental study at The Miami Heart Institute. I'd had a total cholesterol count of nearly fifteen hundred, and the doctors could not determine the cause. Concerned about the elevated lipids, they had placed me on a not-yet federally regulated drug as part of the study. Never before had they tested this drug on a pregnant woman. As soon as I learned of the pregnancy, the doctors advised me to abort the fetus. It seemed the drug company and the institute did not want to assume any liability. In addition, both my obstetrician and internist recommended an abortion. Abortion was not yet legal in Florida in 1971; therefore, I would have to go to New York to have the termination.

My father pleaded with me not to go. He said I would not regret having this child. "Someday you will thank me," he said over and over. "This child will one day bring you more pleasure than you will ever know. Don't do this, Joni. Please, don't do this."

His words branded into my consciousness. They reverberated over and over, resonating with my own feelings.

The day came when we were to go to New York. Paul and I left the house and walked toward the car. My heart ached. I was not comfortable with the decision, even though I had been medically advised to terminate the pregnancy. My brain seemed to accept it, but my heart was weeping.

I stood at the car door and felt compelled to run.

"Get in the car! We're late!" Paul shouted.

I stared at him then at the car door, but was unable to open it.

"No. I can't go through with this. I can't go."

"Get in the car!"

"No. I can't."

Paul came around to my side to put me in the car. Instead, I ran down the street as fast as I could. He chased after me, shouting, "Get in the fucking car! We're going to miss the plane, for God's sake."

Those were the last words I heard. I ran for what seemed to be miles before finding refuge behind a neighbor's lushly landscaped front lawn. I kept hearing my father's voice, "You won't regret this. You are doing the right thing."

I stayed there until I felt certain we would have missed the plane. When I arrived home, Paul was livid. Yet I eventually convinced him that I had done the right thing. Seven months later Aaron was born.

When Aaron was fifteen, he struggled to find his identity, acceptance, and a safe place to share his fears and confusion. I was hardly home. I had been working twelve hours a day, trying to support my children and myself. The child support I received from Paul was insufficient, and by this time my practice had grown.

Nearly a hundred pounds overweight, Aaron's body could not support the changes of his rapid adolescent growth and weight gain. He complained of pain in his knee. It took three weeks to determine the diagnosis, and even then it was wrong. Two doctors misdiagnosed his condition, assuming it was his knee. This resulted in mismanaged treatment that summarily required two eleven-hour surgeries to try to repair a hip fracture due to the weight on Aaron's skeletal structure.

The results had been poor, and over time had worsened to the point that he has never regained full use of his hip and leg. He has a permanent leg differentiation of two inches, which left him with a limp. Now forty, he just recently had a hip replacement as a result of these events.

I glanced up again at Aaron's exquisitely animated face, exceeded only by his imposing presence. The limp he sustained from his accident and subsequent surgeries was obscure as he stood valiantly at the pulpit. His large brown eyes were red and swollen from the tears he shed, yet he wore an appearance of acceptance that none of us were able to embrace. He modeled what we needed to learn. My caboose was pulling the grief for all of us. Today my father's prediction came true!

It's odd how in the midst of tragedy there can be rejoicing. I rejoiced that my children had already become the people they were intended to be. For a few moments, I felt not only proud but also blessed.

My children, all of them, paid homage to their firstborn sister with the same grace and glory as did her girlfriends. My heart was not only filled with sadness but also an unexpected sense of joy. The irony was that in spite of this being the worst day of my life, in some ways it was the best. We were all together, Pam's parents, siblings, colleagues, and friends, saying our final good-bye to this incomparable woman of valor. Yet in this saddest of times I heard the voices of my children exalt their sister with praise and realized that their experiences with her helped mold them into the fine

young adults they had become. Pam had given them a part of her
that would live in their hearts and minds forever.

Now, it was my turn. I looked at Paul and invited him to join
me at the pulpit. His face was contorted with grief. He had gone
pale. His eyes carried anguish and despair. My heart wrenched. I
am sure mine looked no different. We supported each other. He
was unable to speak so I took the microphone. I still don't know
what made it possible to speak the words. I had prepared a short
eulogy the evening before, but I never read it. My heart spoke
instead. All I could think of was the last day I saw her.

The month before we had been celebrating Father's Day with a
brunch Monica had prepared. She had comfortably taken over my
role as hostess for family gatherings as the years wore on.

We were all there—Paul, the children, and even Grandpa Marty,
the kids' only living grandparent. I remember how sad and frumpy
Pam had looked. Her dress was ill fitting and unflattering. She was
no longer the Pam we once knew. That Pam was gone. Only the
shell remained, and even that had decayed. Her depression had
become omnipresent. It was the only face we had seen in the last
few years.

Each of our children presented their father with a gift. Pam
felt ashamed that she, the oldest child, could not afford to buy her
father anything. So in exchange for what could not be purchased,
she read aloud a self-made card. The card was childlike, primitive,

drawn, and written with crayons. But the message said it all. She apologized for what she could not deliver in gifts but hoped her love and appreciation for all he had given her would suffice. There was no gift that could convey her love and devotion. There was nothing money could buy that would express how grateful she felt. She hoped her words would be acceptable and that he knew that her love was no less than the others.

Paul's eyes welled up with tears that quickly escaped down his face. He felt her sense of failure as a daughter. I wonder if he felt his sense of failure as a father. She had always been in the spotlight, exceeding well in every endeavor. This was no longer true. Her sense of esteem and self-worth had eroded as her illness progressed. He too wanted to see the Pam he had once known. Little had we realized that she would be gone in less than a month.

I looked out across the crowded chapel and saw the sad faces that mirrored our own. I'm sure that each parent in the audience knew too well that it easily could have been one of their own children lying in the coffin. No doubt they understood that the grace of God had spared them this wicked fate.

I wanted to make it clear that Pam did not commit suicide. I wanted everyone to know that it was the disease that took her life. I wanted them to know how much she cherished life, her work, her friends, and her family. I wanted them to understand that the illness was her executioner. It was the illness that made the decision. Pam was murdered by a demon who had won a long, tortuous battle. I wanted them to know that it was the illness that stripped from us the life we could have shared. This was surely a woman of valor and a child of God. I was certain she would reside in the house of the Almighty.

Paul tried to speak but the words would not come. His head bent, he wiped the tears coursing his cheeks. He tried to speak to his friends, our loved ones, all who had paid homage to our daughter, but the words stuck behind the lump in his throat. He cleared it, heroically attempting to say what was in his heart, but all he could do was shrug his shoulders, purse his lips, wipe his face with an already soaked handkerchief, and gallantly thank everyone for coming.

We were the first to exit the chapel. The others followed behind. I glanced back and saw a succession of people with hankies and tissues dabbing faces that reflected my own grief. I heard their sobs and cries. They were crying for my loss but one that could have easily been their own, but for the grace of God. The funeral director interrupted my thoughts.

"You and your family will drive in the first limousine, Mrs. Glassman." I was called Mrs. Glassman for the first time in twenty-three years. Once again Paul and I were joined together. We were her parents and she was our daughter and our shared loss.

3

OUR LAST
GOOD-BYE

T he drive to the cemetery seemed to take hours. The
family rode together in a black limousine, traveling
directly behind the hearse. Though I had attended
loved ones' graveside services before, this felt unfamiliar, mostly
because it was my child we were burying, a very different loss
from all the others.

The sky was surreal. Black soot and smoke from the Everglades'
fires lingered in the air, darkening the already overcast sky. The
smoldering heat was relentless. Between the smoke and unbearable
heat, breathing was difficult.

We drove through the cemetery entrance and stopped near the
gravesite, a dozen or more cars followed behind. A tent had been

placed over the open grave that was soon to be her final place on earth. The people gathered around. I looked up at Paul. Bewilderment etched his expression. We moved toward each other clasping hands. We both felt as if we were in a dream, a surrealistic dream.

The rabbi told us what to do every step of the way. He situated me next to Paul, with the children flanked on either side. He recited the customary Hebrew words. The only ones I recognized were names: Pam's, Paul's, and mine. The service began and I stood in a trance observing the people who had come to share our grief and mourning. I watched them yet I didn't really see them. Their faces were a blur. My thoughts took me back to Pam's birth.

Pam came into this world on October 1, 1963, one month and twenty-two days before John Kennedy took that fatal bullet that ended the age of innocence.

It had been an easy pregnancy but a traumatic labor and birth. The pains had begun around midnight on September 29. I gave birth at 1:10 AM on Oct 1. I believe I was in labor more than 24 hours. I stayed awake most of the night. I kept waking Paul, asking him if I was in labor. I was trying to determine if the pains were indeed the first signs of labor. Never having birthed a child before, I was ignorant and scared of the process. By 5:00 AM we got dressed. Paul was on duty at the hospital in Opa-Locka that day. He thought it best I spend the day with him so he could monitor my progress. I should have insisted on going to the hospital where my doctor practiced immediately so I could have him examine me. As I look back, Paul made all the decisions then. I just trusted and obeyed him.

Paul worked every other day and evening at a hospital in Opa-Locka, trying to make some extra money until his practice could sufficiently support us. I spent my labor there until late in the evening, when it was evident that I was close to giving birth. About 10:00 PM, he drove me to another hospital where Pam was to be delivered. I had labored long and hard, more than thirty hours.

Paul stayed with me in the delivery room. My doctor asked me to sit forward so he could administer an epidural. I saw the long needle and panicked. He assured me that it was to numb me from the waist down so I would not have any pain during the delivery. As soon as the needle pierced my lumbar spine, I felt weak and sick. He examined me, then I heard him say that the baby was frank breech—butt first. Because sonograms were not in use to monitor pregnancies in 1963, the breech presentation went undetected.

"We have about ten minutes to get this kid out!" he said, as I lay there on the table, my legs in the stirrups, my body wrapped in sheets, scared out of my wits that something might go wrong. I was not yet twenty-four years old. I tasted my salty tears as they ran down my cheeks. I tried to be brave. I began to slip away into some kind of altered state, somewhere between consciousness and semi-consciousness. I felt like I was falling into an abyss. I glanced at the clock: 1:10 AM.

"It's coming. Push, Joni, push!" I heard the words, but they seemed far away, like they were not for me. "Push harder. We need your help."

The doctor called to me. Paul called to me and I heard the doctor. I heard Paul. Then I heard her cry. I heard them say, "It's a girl!"

"It's a girl, and she looks just like me!" Paul said.

I slipped deeper into the abyss, in shock from an allergic reaction to the epidural. I woke up two days later with Ace bandages wrapped around every part of my body, like a mummy. Shock blocks had been placed under my bed to raise me to increase my blood pressure.

Paul was standing next to me when I opened my eyes. "Thank God," he said. He looked terrified. I noticed a deep scowl creviced between his eyes that had never been there before.

"I thought we were going to lose you. You went into shock. You had an allergic reaction to the epidural. We have a daughter and she looks like me!"

The rabbi saying the Kaddish—the Jewish commemoration prayer for the deceased—startled me to the present. I had heard that haunting melody and words so many times before for others. And now I was hearing it for my daughter.

"Yisgadal v'yiskadash shmai raba."

This can't be happening. This is Kaddish. My daughter is dead. I held Paul's hand, fixated on Pam's casket embossed in the center with a Jewish star. It was the same style casket I had chosen to hold my mother's body five years before. I felt weak, as if my legs wouldn't hold me. The suffocating heat sapped what little strength I possessed. I thought I was going to faint.

Control yourself. Just control yourself. Be strong for the children. They need you now. Just hold on. I suppose I was really trying to be strong for myself. I managed to stay focused as the heat and the ceremony seemed to strip me of the ability to breathe.

I looked over at my children. Their faces were pale, almost ashen. *How will they ever recover? How will they get past this? What guilt do they carry? Just shut up! Just shut up!* I said over and over again to myself. I didn't want these thoughts, but they came unbidden. How are we going to survive this?

The coffin slowly lowered into the grave. The chains that cradled the coffin creaked as it worked its way down. I glanced into the dark pit and saw water at the bottom. Oh, my God. She's going to lie in water. Moans and cries of my children distracted me. Then a chorus of voices joined in.

The rabbi sprinkled some earth from Israel onto the coffin as it touched down to rest. He spoke again. He spoke first in Hebrew then repeated in English: "Ashes to ashes, dust to dust." Then he recited the twenty-third Psalm. "The Lord is my shepherd; I shall not want. He maketh me to lie down in green pastures ..." We stood in those green pastures and watched as Pam's casket was lowered into the ground; it would soon be part of the earth that would cover her grave.

How many times had she recited this psalm in the past two years? How many times had she asked me to recite it? She carried the Old Testament with her wherever she went. In an effort to move closer to God, she had become pious these last two years, hoping that by giving herself to God, he would save her.

I faded out, recalling Israel, the last trip Pam and I took together less than a year before the funeral.

In December 1997, a few months after Chava had gone through stem cell replacement, she had asked me to attend her daughter's wedding in Tel Aviv. While Chava lay desperately sick in the hospital, she still managed to plan her daughter's wedding.

Pam pleaded to join me. She believed that if she could be in the Holy Land, praying by the Wailing Wall every day in Jerusalem, God would save her from the Devil. I thought it preposterous, but after much deliberation, I agreed to take her along.

The trip was a nightmare. Pam left her medication in Miami, hoping I would not discover her intentional subterfuge. She had always been resistant to taking her medications, as are many patients with the same illness. She believed that the medications were agents of the Devil and were part of a conspiracy to take her soul.

The long flight was unbearable. It was after two days of trying to keep her feeling safe from her delusions that I learned she had not brought her medications with her. Luckily, my girlfriend's family found a psychiatrist in Tel Aviv who immediately filled a prescription. I was not convinced that Pam ever took it. She had mastered some foolproof deceptions.

The days that followed were horrendous. Pam believed that Tel Aviv was an underground duplication of the real city created by the Devil to fool us. Using a Hebrew prayer book, which I didn't know she could read, she prayed fervently, passionately, and desperately five times a day. Clutching the prayer book, she faced east, bowing and chanting the prayers as if she had done this all her life.

Each day we boarded a bus to Jerusalem so she could visit and pray by the wall. She begged me to stay in the Old City so she could surround herself with those she believed could protect and help her. She convinced me to stay for a weekend with a religious family who had eleven children. She wanted to celebrate the Sabbath with them, convinced that God would look upon her with mercy and redeem her soul. Chava's family made the arrangements.

We spent the Sabbath, Friday evening to Saturday evening, with Rachel and Nasaniel, their eleven children, and their niece and nephew. Rachel and Nasaniel were American Jews originally from Brooklyn. Their eldest child was not yet sixteen and the youngest was an infant. Both of them were only thirty-four. We slept in a hall bedroom that was barely the size of a closet. They had only one bathroom to accommodate all fifteen of us.

Pam shared her fears with Nasaniel, who taught the Torah. He tried to console her with his teachings and good intentions, hoping she would accept his word. She tried. She went to the synagogue five times a day, worshipping upstairs where the women prayed.

We joined this family for the Sabbath lunch and dinner. I wanted to leave and get back to my own reality, for I thought I was going to lose my mind. But Pam pleaded again to spend the night and leave Sunday. They encouraged us to stay, so I agreed. I felt helpless, powerless, and desperate.

Chava was in the hospital near Tel Aviv. I wanted to be with her too. My heart was torn between the two of them.

We celebrated Chanukah (Hanukkah) that week. Each night, whether we were in the hospital with Chava, in the streets of Tel Aviv or Jerusalem, or in the home of Nasaniel and Rachel, we lit a candle. Each night I said a prayer. "Please help my daughter. Please, dear God, take this disease from her. Give her back her life. Please let Chava live. Don't take her from me. Let her live."

Sometimes I forgot who needed the prayers more—them or me. I was in a state of panic. I spent my days sharing woes between a dying girlfriend and my disturbed and panic-stricken daughter. Each night she cried, "Hold me, Mommy. Hold me and pray for me."

I had no answers, nothing to offer, yet I held her in my arms, promising not to let anything or anyone hurt her—a promise I could not keep for long.

In the evenings, close to midnight, we walked the streets of Tel Aviv. We marched militantly holding our fists in the air, shouting, "I defy you! I defy you! I won't accept you or your power!" Over and over we proclaimed the refrain. I tried to help her by sharing in her determination to win. She tried. She really tried, but the disease was winning and I was losing my daughter. Her eyes were vacuous. She stared but never looked at anything. Her smile had vanished. Her face was contorted with fear and impending doom. She cried all the time. Her tears were a part of who she was becoming. My heart was so heavy. I wanted to help but could offer no answers, no solutions, and no cure.

Pam's religiosity had no boundaries. She visited the Christian and Muslim quarters so she could pray to Jesus and Allah, respectively. I couldn't make sense out of any of it. I just tried to comfort her and fulfill all her wishes.

We followed the steps of the Via Dolorosa through the narrow alleys to the Church of the Holy Sepulchre. She kissed each spot where Jesus had stopped to rest and kissed the sacred altar that marked the spot of his burial. We traveled to Bethlehem to visit his birthplace, the Church of the Nativity. We walked the steps where monks sat at water holes to signify where the Christ Child had been bathed. We bathed in both the Dead Sea and the Jordan River so she could feel cleansed from the evil she felt had invaded her spirit.

She wanted to visit Yad Veshem, the memorial to the Holocaust, so she could pray for the souls of the men, women, and children who had been lost to atrocities of the Nazis. She cried as if she personally had known each and every one of them. She intimated that in some way she felt responsible for their demise.

Each day was another impassioned sojourn. We traveled to Masada where we ascended the cable to the fortress built by Herod and where Jews had taken their own lives to escape capture by the Romans. She prayed at every possible prayer site, including the ancient synagogue. She bowed her head into the palm of her hand as she crouched in despair, hoping against hope, looking for answers that never came.

There seemed to be no end to her search for release from her inner demons. Wherever we traveled, she stopped to pray in every church and synagogue along the way, hoping she would be heard and healed. She looked for answers wherever we traveled and spoke to anyone who seemed interested or knowledgeable. No matter what they said, no matter what words of encouragement they spoke, she walked away feeling hopeless. She felt doomed and there was nothing I could do about it.

In spite of the worst two weeks of my life, caught between a dying friend and a sick daughter, I managed to attend the wedding. Pam looked beautiful as always, but her affect was gone. Her spirit had faded. The beauty that had once radiated from within had vanished. Only a shell of loveliness remained.

Against her doctor's orders, Chava attended her daughter's wedding. She hired an ambulance with two paramedics to take her to the wedding hall. Climbing the steps taxed every ounce of will and strength. She was breathless by the time she reached the top. We embraced as she made it onto the landing, weeping in each other's arms. Her fight was so admirable. She was so amazing, so beautiful, in spite of the illness and medications' disfiguring effects of her face and body. Even in her dying state, barely able to breathe and carry herself up the staircase, she maintained her beauty, dignity, and inner strength.

The wedding was like life itself: tragedy and joy intertwined. The music played, we danced, ate, and for a few moments we forgot the realities of our lives. Chava saw her daughter marry. Three months later Chava died.

By the time we had left Israel, Pam was nearly catatonic. I had feared they might have to land the plane mid-flight to hospitalize her. By the grace of God we had made it home, whereupon she once again had to be hospitalized.

The rabbi handed the shovel to me. "Here, take this. Throw some earth on it before we cover the casket." I was stunned. I didn't want to bury my own daughter. I didn't want to shovel any dirt on top of her resting place. It seemed almost barbaric. I looked at him with horror.

"It's okay," he whispered. "It's okay. It's our tradition."

Suddenly I realized how little I knew about our tradition. I was sure I didn't like this. I reluctantly reached for the shovel and dug into the ground to lift the dirt. I threw it on the coffin and then dug again. Each of us, one by one, followed suit.

The rabbit offered Pam's friends the opportunity to do the same. A few came forward. They gathered around me. One young woman, who had been a friend since childhood, held the shovel in her hand. Tears ran down her cheeks.

"Why did this happen to her?" she cried. "Pam loved everyone. She was so special, like an angel."

"She was an angel," I said. "And how lucky we were to have been touched by her life. I feel so privileged for having been chosen as her mother."

Only later that evening while humming a song did the implication of my words hit me.

4

THAT SAME EVENING

I arrived home from the funeral and cemetery still in a daze. I was exhausted. I took off my black suit, which by now felt like a sweatsuit. The smell of perspiration from the heat of the day coupled with the pulling it out of the hamper that morning was unbearable. I barely recognized myself when I saw my reflection in the mirror. I looked drawn and old, like I had aged ten years in two days.

I stepped into a hot shower, washing off as much of the day as possible. I let the water fall on my face, as if to rinse away my sorrow and bring me back to days long past. I wished we could begin again. I began humming an old melody. As the water splashed on my face, my voice rang out. I faded to another memory that brought back what I had uttered only a few hours before at the gravesite.

When Pam was only a few months old, we had lived in a one-bedroom apartment in Miami Beach. Paul worked long hours while I stayed home caring for our daughter. I cradled her in awe of the miracle that I had given birth to this amazing little girl, yet I had very little to do with the process. Her conception and birth had been entirely God's will.

We had been trying for months and were told that I would have a difficulty in conceiving due to an inverted uterus. Her conception was a gift. It came from some divine order and I reveled that I was the mother of this perfect child.

A song was born out of this miracle. I sang it to her every day. When she was ten months old, we moved into our first home. I purchased an antiquated, junked, baby grand piano from the local Jewish Home for the Aged.

One evening, I sat at the piano and wrote down the notes to a melody I had been humming since her birth. I titled it "The Face of an Angel." The words had come so easily to me.

> *This is the face of an angel,*
> *Sent here from heaven above.*
> *This is the face of an angel,*
> *Sent here for me to love.*
> *Hair of gold like an angel,*
> *Eyes of green like the sea,*

And this face of an angel,
Soon will belong to me.
When God made the angels in heaven above,
He told them that everyone would fall in love.
And this little angel he chose to be,
The one who'd fall in love with me.
Now that my story is over,
Here's what I'm hoping will be,
That this little face of an angel
Soon will belong to me.

I sang it over and over while the shower washed away the events of the day. I sensed that Pam had been trying to communicate with me. She had been singing through me. I sang the song that I had written and sung to her more than thirty-four years before. The lyrics and melody came to me as if I had sung them every day of my life, yet so much time had passed since I had even thought about it. The song had remained in my subconscious.

Pam was whispering the words back into my consciousness. She was indeed an angel. I didn't know back then that I would give birth to an angel. I didn't believe angels existed. I thought of them as a projection of some divine belief of fundamentalists, the orthodox, religious zealots, or New Age fanatics. I saw them as fantasies in the movies, wishful or magical childhood beliefs, or ornaments to don the tops of Christmas trees. In other words, angels didn't exist. The thought of conceiving an angel was anathema to me.

I wrapped the towel around my naked body and went into my bedroom. On the dresser next to all the other photos sat a recent photo of Pam. I looked at her. "Thank you, sweetheart," I whispered. "Thank you for choosing me."

5

Shiva: Seven Days of Mourning

Day One: Pam's Dream

The week my daughter died, we sat shiva (a Jewish ritual of seven days for mourning the deceased) in her father's apartment, the same apartment from which she'd leaped to her death. The setting was difficult for us. That window confronted us every day, reminding us of her jump onto the concrete fifteen stories below. Located in Bal Harbour, Florida, the building overlooked the
Atlantic Ocean. Pam had placed a chair by the window and sat, gazing out for a long time. And now it gazed back at us.

I still did not know the events of that day. I was too preoccupied with the onslaught of activities surrounding her sudden death. I needed to ask. But I was afraid to learn the truth. I had procrastinated and thought I would ask her father later. Now was not an appropriate time.

According to the Jewish religion, it is important to hold the shiva where the deceased was last alive. They say that the soul is present for seven days. Not knowing if this was accurate and not having the strength to challenge it, I subjugated my feelings about changing the venue to my home and reluctantly accepted the decision her father made.

The apartment was filled with family, friends, and food. The limited space made it difficult to handle such a large crowd. The mornings were quiet; but by late afternoon, people came in droves.

I thought that while it was still morning and the apartment was vacant of any outsiders, I would share my revelation about the song with the family. Before I could complete my story, Paul and my other grown children burst into tears as they had remembered the song that had not been sung in many years.

The sensation that had entered my body the night before while showering and remembering Pam's song remained in full bloom, except I was able to disassociate it from my internal cues. I seemed calm, almost elated, as if nothing had happened.

I looked out that window and tried to imagine what could have entered her mind as she made the decision to jump. I tried to concoct a reason, a rationale. But how could I enter the mind of a disturbed person? How would I ever know?

The window continued to haunt me. The mental video kept playing over and over; the window seemed to trigger the play button. In my mind, images flashed of Pam dressed in a particular outfit, though I didn't know what she had worn that day. I imagined her seeing something either very frightening or very inviting, beckoning her toward the window or scaring her through the window. What might have happened? What could have made her do this? What had she seen or heard that provoked her to jump?

"My poor baby. My poor, poor baby," I said again and again, hardly audible. But the words were loud to my ears.

I asked Paul if she had left a note of any kind. Had he found some thread of evidence that she was going to take her life? He said that she had written something, but it was about the dream she'd had the night before. I asked to see it.

He brought me her yellow legal pad. With a sense of wonder, I read what she had written. The first paragraph was easy to read. The handwriting had been quite legible.

July 2, 1998

Dream

I was with my grandpa at some apartment.

I was packing to go somewhere.

To drive around a mountain.

He thought in a knowing, sinister way that he would . . .

The second paragraph shifted in character. Although still legible, it took more effort to read.

But I went into another room and got a cane with a paper towel wrapped around it. I felt I would be safe. I was nervous, but was feeling more secure to leave.

Then, there was a bus scene. Grandpa Gene (her maternal grandfather) was there with Grandma Dorothy (her paternal grandmother, both deceased).

Erika and I were on the bus. They were glad to have me with them. Erika was driving. I complimented her. She had been such an angel through this. So had my grandfather, Gene. They said something about Aaron having to play sinister. But I was on my way back home with them. They haven't let go.

By the time I was halfway down the page, the scrawl was such that I was unable to make out half the words.

I want to document what happened with the angels and saints today. I saw a rescue truck at 2500 E. Hallandale Beach Blvd, my mom's office. I had the thought that I kept getting rescued, but when am I going to give back? I was able to bless someone in the elevator and . . .

The words ran off the page. I was unable to understand any more.

Perhaps it was in that moment she lost contact with reality. I, of course, will never know what happened. I can only assume. My guess was that she saw or heard something so frightening that she ran away from the perceived threat, or that perhaps she saw her grandparents waiting by the window, beckoning to take her home. She might have heard them call to her, as the dream suggested. I would like to believe that it was this that she saw. The torment is that I will never really know the truth.

That evening after the first day of shiva concluded with the ritual Kaddish service, the service for the dead, I returned home. I stepped into the shower again. I hoped the water would take away my pain as well as the heat of the day. I cried. Anger bubbled from deep within. My rage overcame my state of sorrow. It hemorrhaged from me.

"I can't believe you would do such a thing, Pam!" I shouted. "Damn you, damn you, you bitch. Why? Why? You had no right! You could have told me. I just spoke to you on Tuesday. Why didn't you tell me? I asked you if you were suicidal! You told me you would never leave such a legacy. You lied, you lied! How could you?"

Then I heard her voice, as if she were in the shower with me.

"I didn't do it, Mom. It's not my fault. God came and saved me. He wanted me not to suffer. He took me home. Please, I need you to forgive me. I need you to understand."

I was quiet. I heard her. I was listening but unable to realize that she was here with me. My fury was not yet spent.

"I hate you. I hate you! You didn't have to do this! What are we going to do?"

Again, she spoke, inside my head. But I heard her as if she were standing next to me.

"Mom, I'm here. I am here with you. But I had to go. I was in so much pain. I needed peace. I needed peace. Please, don't be mad. I love you. I love all of you."

I cried out loud. This surrealistic dialogue with my daughter unnerved me. I could hear her inside my head.

"Mom, go to the window tomorrow. I will give you a sign. Go there at 11:00 AM. Look out the window."

I screamed.

DAY 2: PAM'S SIGN

I hated that window. But I was drawn to it. I didn't feel in charge of my own will. Pam's summon compelled me to go to the window.

I arrived at Paul's apartment before 11:00 AM. I wandered toward the window and looked at the same view Pam had seen only three days before. The ocean was calm with the exception of a few rolling waves cresting onto the shoreline. There were scattered cumulous clouds loomed low in an otherwise blue sky.

I tried to imagine what her sign to me would be. I waited. I watched. I saw nothing unusual, nothing that made any impact on me. Sea gulls dove for their breakfast. A few people strolled along the boardwalk and on the beach. The construction crew below noisily tore up the concrete. A whirring sound generated by a bulldozer reminded me that life goes on. The construction crew had witnessed her jump. They had called 9-1-1.

I saw no signs. Maybe I was losing my own reality. What did I expect? Was I going crazy?

"Move away from there, Mom. Why are you standing there?" one of my children said.

I was afraid to tell them why. It would have upset them even more.

"I will. I just need to be here a few more minutes. Just give me a little more time." I noticed some sea gulls flying by the window. Why did they pick this floor? Why the fifteenth floor? I watched them, curious as to why they had landed atop the building facing me. There were five all in a row. They stood there for what might have been a minute or so, but long enough for me to notice them. Suddenly, one flew away. The others remained.

Could this have been her sign? Was this her way of telling me that she was home? For some reason, it didn't matter. I sensed a shift in my internal state and I felt better. I silently thanked her for the message, then went back to the family.

My son Todd and his wife had been visiting us during the last week of June. Having been given only one week of vacation, he'd had to return to his residency in Ohio. His wife had stayed to be with her mother until the end of July. Of course, Todd had been called back the following week for the funeral and shiva. It was during that week that they conceived their first child.

God gives and God takes. Was that another sign? Was that an affirmation of God's will? Was God trying to make up for taking Pam? Was this his way of distracting us from our loss by blessing us with a granddaughter? I yearned to keep Pam with me, and many times I wondered if Pam's soul returned to us in our grandchild. I tried not to think about it, but despite my rejections, it kept invading my thoughts. The thought was a double-edged blade, both hopeful and yet macabre. It both frightened me and pleased me. But I was able to welcome my first grandchild, Jacqueline, into this world as her own being.

DAYS THREE THROUGH SEVEN

The rest of the week felt like unnumbered pages in a book. One day followed another. Each day began the same way, felt the same, and ended the same. And each day redefined my new reality. People came. People stayed. People gave their condolences. People ate with us. People prayed with us. People mourned with us.

We covered the mirrors (another Jewish custom that prohibits the mourners from viewing themselves). The spirit of shiva had to remain pure. One had to be devoted to prayer and mourning without concern of appearances. The men ceased shaving. The women wore no makeup. The self was not important, only the honoring of the dead. Everyone grew weary. Each evening and sometimes twice in the evening, the men gathered with the women behind them, separated at the time of services, chanting the ritual Kaddish. The apartment began to take on its own personality. It had become a mecca for mourners. The mood hung heavy with sadness and grief.

As I stood among my family and friends, I stumbled over the Hebrew words I did not understand. I held the prayer book that included the English transliteration. The words looked foreign. They sounded foreign, even though I had heard them many times in my past. This was different. These words were for the mourning of my daughter. I could not concentrate. I kept envisioning her leap onto the concrete. I tried to distract myself. I tried to remember when her illness began.

The first sign that had alerted us to a serious illness had come in October 1989, when she was twenty-four years old. I had been preparing for a four-day conference with John Bradshaw, a well-known leader in the field of recovery and Pam's employer. In fact, it was through her employment that John and I created a professional association.

At the young age of twenty-two, Pam began working as a clinical therapist at the John Bradshaw Center in Los Angeles. The work at the center focused on second-stage recovery. John Bradshaw's book and television series, *Bradshaw: On the Family*, launched John's career nationally, and he brought the recovery movement to its highest level of recognition. He became a leading authority nationwide on recovery. Most of the patients in this program had been traumatized as children with abuse, neglect, or abandonment. They acted out in addictive behaviors. Many were recovering alcoholics, drug addicts, and they suffered from severe codependency issues, including sex and love addictions. The methods used to help the patients discharge their unexpressed emotions were highly experiential. In helping patients release these feelings, the energy can be absorbed by an inexperienced therapist whose boundaries are not secure enough to contain the discharged energy. Because of her youth and inexperience, combined with her predisposition to bipolar disorder, Pam was vulnerable and susceptible to receiving the patients' negative energy.

John and I had been working for months on a four-day seminar on "The Wounded Inner Child." One day my phone rang. I answered it, not knowing that my life was about to take a dramatic shift.

Pam had lived with two other girls in an apartment in Los Angeles. They were calling to tell me that they had just brought her home from the emergency room.

"We're worried about Pam. She's acting strange. She's sick and we think she needs to go home."

Pam's other roommate, Velda, who was on the extension, said, "We think she needs help and we don't know what to do."

Velda briefly explained that Pam had been exhibiting paranoia. Pam had disclosed to her roommates that seven strange people, all of whom were wearing black and chanting her name, were stalking her. They beckoned her to come with them. In her fragile state, she lost control and ran through the neighborhood, screaming like a helpless child. She was terrorized by what was probably her first hallucination. I believe this event was triggered by smoking marijuana, something she had never done before. Drugs can precipitate a paranoid state and produce hallucinations, especially if the user has a predisposition to mental illness.

Her roommates had called 9-1-1. The paramedics transported Pam to the emergency room of the nearest hospital. When the doctor examined her and learned of her drug episode, he quickly dismissed her irrational behavior as a response to the drug. He released Pam to her friends, but she continued to hallucinate. This had prompted the call.

Two days later I received a second call from another girlfriend.

"Hi, this is Ellen, Pam's friend."

"Is anything wrong, Ellen?" I was afraid to hear what I feared would not be good.

"She hasn't bathed or washed her hair for several days. She appears disoriented. She can hardly complete a sentence. It's like she's in a trance or altered state."

"Let me talk to Pam, please."

Ellen got Pam on the phone.

"Honey, how are you feeling?"

It was as Ellen had described. Pam was incoherent, her responses disjointed.

I determined that it would be too difficult to handle this situation long-distance, so I wanted to bring Pam to Miami to be with me. I called her supervisor at the center and asked him to check on her and assess if she was capable of flying alone. A few hours later he called to confirm that she was quite disoriented. He believed that the best treatment would be for her to be with me. Ellen put her on a plane the next day.

Her father and I met her at the airport in Miami. She was bewildered, mistrustful, and frightened as we approached her. Her hair was dirty, her clothes disheveled, and she appeared disoriented. It was obvious she was very ill.

"Mom," she cried, "the people, the people . . . the people on the p-p-plane . . ." Then she paused and stared at me without recognition.

"What? What are you saying?" I tried to get her to focus.

Her eyes were vacuous. "The people on the plane . . ."

"Go on," I pleaded.

"Moving . . . moving in slow motion," she stammered. She couldn't complete a sentence. Her affect was frozen. She looked as if she had seen a ghost.

"I have seen the other side," she whispered.

Confused, frightened, and not knowing what to do, we did our best to calm her, but she kept repeating over and over, "I have seen the other side."

Her disorientation to time, person, and place indicated that she was falling apart. It was clear she was suffering from mental illness. She had seen several psychiatrists and psychologists but none had ever diagnosed her with bipolar disorder, and she had never received effective treatment.

From birth, Pam's behaviors had been different from my friends' babies. I realize now that Pam exhibited extremes since early infancy. Because she was my first child, I had no practical frame of reference or comparison. Mealtimes were a disaster. She was messy. Unlike other babies who dribble food out of their mouths, Pam often spat out her food. She played in her food and often threw it onto the floor, so that by the end of each feeding, it looked like a train had roared through the dining area. Until almost two years of age, she made messes with her feces, using it as clay or putty, applying it to the sides of the crib and onto the walls. It became a daily ritual to wash down the crib and walls after bathing and dressing her. Her playtime mirrored her eating behavior. She tossed her toys everywhere. Nothing was in its place. I thought she would grow out of these behaviors, but instead they worsened. Every day was painstakingly difficult.

As she grew, so did the bad habits. She seemed to be happiest in chaos. I had to urge her daily to clean up after herself, to tell her to shower and care for her personal items. In her teen years, her mood and attitude turned surly and depressed. During her adolescence, I began to consider that perhaps a mental disorder was lurking, but she compensated so well in other ways that it was difficult to identify. During the sixties and seventies, mental disorders were not as clearly defined and diagnosed. Today, it would be very clear that she would fall somewhere on the spectrum.

Her compensation had been so effective that her symptoms eluded everyone close to her. In fact, she was adored by her siblings, grandparents, and friends. No teacher had ever called me in for a conference to discuss any deviant or unmanageable behaviors. Even if I had recognized Pam's behaviors as symptoms of something more serious, I was too close to the situation to really understand the implications.

It wasn't until 1975 that I entered my first year of social work at Barry College. Thus my knowledge about these things was minimal. In addition, as her mother and primary custodian, I was probably in denial. Her father had been living in Missouri during these years and was not present to share the parenting role with me.

Pam knew how to fool us all, and this lasted up until the time the disease manifested into a full-blown manic episode. However, signs appeared during her college years—that her roommates later shared with me—as well as through stories I heard from my aunt with whom Pam had lived with during the year she attended Adelphi to obtain her master's degree in social work. My aunt reported that her room was always in disarray. Pam would stuff her clothes under her bed and shove them in the closet rather than hanging them up and caring for them properly. This really bothered my aunt because she knew how hard it was for me to bear the responsibility of providing Pam with a wardrobe and to help her financially during this time.

My aunt also shared other horror stories about the men Pam would bring over while trying to inhibit her from noticing. She also told me that Pam would light candles at night against her wishes, once starting a fire that my aunt was thankfully able to extinguish. This was the year that her illness could no longer be disguised. Pam's behavior toward me was openly aggressive, and often her behavior toward others was inappropriate and/or bizarre as well.

By now, in her early twenties, her illness had manifested. After going out to Los Angeles and securing her position as a therapist at the John Bradshaw Center, her mental status deteriorated beyond recognition. Due to her enormous ability to compensate and her talent as a therapist, her clients adored her, but the more they improved, the worse she became. It wasn't until a conference in 1989 that I sponsored in South Florida that her first breakdown occurred.

Paul and I admitted her to a psychiatric facility the next morning known as The Retreat, a comprehensive in-patient center where the psychiatrist diagnosed her as having a Manic Disorder and a Psychotic break. The psychiatrist who treated her at that time had not yet given Pam a bipolar diagnosis. He put her on an antidepressant and an antipsychotic drug. She responded almost immediately. Her recovery was amazing. At this point, while I had been in private practice for eleven years, I had never diagnosed or treated anyone with a bipolar disorder and was not familiar enough with it.

Both the doctor and I urged Pam to set aside the last semester of her PhD program at her school in LA to stay home, but her sense of urgency to get back trumped our pleading. I was in a state of panic. I knew she would have another episode if she didn't give herself adequate time to heal.

At that time, we were not aware of her fear regarding the school's losing its license to continue with the doctorate program. Because the school was shutting its doors at the conclusion of the semester, she had to attend to earn her degree.

Her father supported her decision, unaware of the implications of the illness. He minimized the seriousness of the disorder.
Albeit a physician, he knew nothing about mental illness and was
in major denial. He saw only what he wanted to see. Adding to
her pressure of her school closing, Pam felt obliged to please her
father by finishing her doctorate program.

Discharged from the hospital two weeks later, as though nothing
had ever happened, Pam looked and acted her usual self. We were
relieved, but I was suspicious that our battle wasn't over.

While Pam had not yet been diagnosed with bipolar disorder,
given our professional knowledge and experiences with patients, we
had every reason to fear that we were looking at the same illness.
We wanted Pam to wait a few months before going back to California. We had felt that she was still too fragile and needed more
time to heal. But she was adamant and insisted on returning to LA.

After learning of her hospitalization, the John Bradshaw Center
recognized just how ill Pam really was and dismissed her. She had
worked alongside John since the center's inception and helped write
the treatment program that they implemented there. But regardless
of the success Pam had had with her clients, they feared she was
not strong enough to do the experiential abreaction work she had
been assigned. Her supervisor determined that her boundaries had
been compromised. Her dismissal threw her into a shame spiral.
Her fragile ego could not tolerate the center's rejection. She felt
betrayed and deeply hurt. They were concerned about the liability
regarding their patients and had to cover their bases. I don't blame

them—the dismissal was intended to protect both the patients and her—but it was too painful for her to accept.

Pam needed to work to support herself, so she opted to go into private practice. She quickly expanded to two office locations. Many of the patients released from the center followed her for after care. Her reputation as a wizard therapist traveled quickly. She journeyed between Santa Monica and Long Beach, running groups and filling in at the John Bradshaw Center whenever they needed her. While the center felt that Pam's mental status was too impaired to work full time, they allowed her to fill in on group sessions when other therapists were absent. She was a master of group therapy and thus they felt assured she had enough ego boundaries and strengths to handle this.

Pam seemed to have successfully reentered normal life, but it was short lived. The disease grew insidiously in her brain, weaving a path that was destined to kill her. She disguised the symptoms by over-compensating, a defense she had mastered.

Against the doctor's advice, Pam continued to go to graduate school for her PhD. Because it had lost its funding, the school's nonaccredited evening program was now pushing the students through. It needed to graduate this last class in less than a year and Pam felt unprepared to receive a PhD. She did not believe she'd earned it according to her standards; therefore, she was never proud of it. She felt like a fraud, ashamed of saying where she earned it. She never once used it. Her certificate always read, Pamela Ann Glassman, LCSW, which was her professional status prior to her post-graduate degree.

Her father was proud. He had financed her education and had encouraged her to continue and matriculate in spite of her condition. He never really understood how ill she was. He didn't want to believe that Pam was suffering from a mental disorder. There is no doubt in my mind that if he understood how ill she really was, he would not have been so eager for her to continue. She wanted to please him, and she felt he would be angry and disappointed if she did not finish.

Prior to her hospitalization, paranoid behaviors intensified as Pam's illness took hold. She had met Josef at an Inner Child Workshop she and other staff therapists were facilitating with John Bradshaw. I was visiting her at the time and attended the workshop to learn more about John's presentation and content. Her attraction to an attendee, a very handsome Middle Eastern man, became apparent. She paid too much attention to him during the workshop, and I had to remind her a few times that she was there to be a support therapist, not to be flirting with one of the participants. But Pam's behavior was ruled by her underlying, not-yet-diagnosed illness. One of the symptoms of bipolar disorder is promiscuous, flirtatious behavior. She made it obvious to anyone who was paying attention to her that she was smitten with Josef. That same evening, she invited him to her apartment.

With her flirtatious, wanton behavior, being there as her house guest and mother created an awkward situation. She had nothing in her apartment that would allow her to entertain guests, not even a cup to drink from, so I suggested we buy some supplies so she could serve Josef tea or coffee and some cookies. She hadn't a clue to think of this obvious gesture on her own.

Their meeting turned into a six-month relationship that morphed into an engagement. Pam brought him home to meet the family. Josef was a poor, Jewish immigrant from Iran struggling to make a living and find his way in America. Perhaps she was a ticket to his advantage, but it didn't appear that way when I saw them together. He seemed as crazy about her as she was for him. Josef had no money for an engagement ring, so I offered mine as a wedding present, knowing that she would want and need what all engaged girls have—a ring. He accepted my offer, and they went together to select a new setting. Her father threw a beautiful engagement party for them at a local Greek restaurant he frequented, inviting perhaps two hundred guests. She and her father danced the customary *Hasapiko* and other traditional Greek folk dances before the guests. He had taught her these dances during the years after our divorce and loved dancing with Pam. She was the only daughter who had adopted his hobby.

Everything looked wonderful and we began making wedding plans. After the party, the couple went back to Los Angeles where Josef returned to his job as an engineer and Pam as a therapist at the center.

Then she began calling me, telling of her suspicions that Josef was cheating on her. She lamented that he hadn't come home the previous night, that his once voracious sexual interest in her had disappeared, and that it was evident that he no longer had interest in her as a future wife. He would often scold her for her uninhabitable housekeeping skills, her lack of hygiene, and many other behaviors he found offensive. She generally responded to him in anger, then he'd ignore her and walk out, leaving her alone to deal with her anger and disappointment. When she confronted Josef with her suspicions, he denied them, often deleting or distorting information. She was a sleuth, ready to attack; he retreated and withdrew, which exacerbated her behavior, making her more suspicious.

Their relationship eroded over time, but he was not aware of how bad her mental status had deteriorated. I knew there were issues. I knew about her lack of housekeeping, her ineptness with household responsibilities, but not living there, it was hard for me to judge how much she contributed to the demise of their relationship and his reasons for acting out. Looking back, I can understand how he might have become disinterested in her—even turned off. She was not easy to be with, let alone live with.

Pam would often rant and wail about her feelings, most often blaming others for her unhappiness—another sign of the illness. One was always in a double bind with Pam. Her feelings of displeasure, even contempt, were often laden with feelings of love and affection. Often, I felt as if I was with two different people. I never knew when or how she would react. The signs of illness were there at least a few years before the engagement, but they were concealed so well with her ability to compensate and camouflage those negative traits with tenderness, intelligence, and genuine caring that clarity was never there. It drove those of us who were close to her crazy.

Josef finally called it quits after many confrontations regarding his womanizing, neglect of her, and staying out all night. She had no other choice except to terminate the engagement. He appeared relieved. His side of the story was that she was too difficult to live with. Her inability to take care of the apartment as well as her excessive weight gain, combined with her rapid mood swings, violent outbursts, and sloppiness caused him to lose interest in her.

This loss came at a precarious time as her mental state and self-esteem had already been severely compromised with her hospitalization and the loss of her job as a full-time therapist at the center, which had meant so much to her. In addition, she was exhausted trying to complete the doctorate program while building her private practice. Josef had been the most important person in her life. Their breakup coupled with all her other losses led to her next breakdown.

My last thought before the refrains from the Kaddish service interrupted my memories was that it took the earthquakes and her final return to Florida to shatter the remainder of her existence.

Everyone in unison said, "Amen."

THE DAY SHE JUMPED

The next morning began like all the others. The trays of food arrived around 11:00 AM. It was quiet at this time. My children were not there yet. Most of the guests came after their workdays.

I had never learned exactly what had happened. I was so caught up in the events of the death, funeral, and shiva that I didn't even ask.

Paul and I sat on the sofa in the living room. He looked haggard. It seemed as if he'd aged overnight. Where there once were strands of gray in his hair, it had now turned white. His eyes were still swollen. They seemed to sink into his hallowed brows. We'd both lost weight in a very brief amount of time.

I asked him if he wanted a cup a tea. He didn't acknowledge my offer. I went to the kitchen and brought him some tea. As I handed him the cup, I asked the question I had been afraid to ask yet needed to know.

"What happened that day?"

He paused, rolled his eyes upward as if he were making pictures in his mind. He sat the teacup on the coffee table and placed his hand over his mouth as if he did not want to form the words. Then he spoke very quietly.

"Pam," he whispered, "Pam was writing something on the dining room table when I was about to leave for work. I asked her what she was writing. She told me it was her dream."

He was referring to the dream I had read the day before.

"I thought nothing of it and asked her what her plans were for the day. She told me she was going to meet Dina, Todd's wife, for lunch. They were going together to her psychiatrist. Afterward they were going to have lunch and go to the beach."

He looked directly into my eyes. I saw his sorrow as if it were my own.

"I asked her if she needed any money. I wrote a check for her to take to the auto mechanic for her air-conditioner. I gave her some ties to take to Dina that Todd had left behind when he was here just last week."

He went on to tell me that his girlfriend, Astrid, had broken her leg just a few days before, so she was resting on the bed in their master bedroom. He had seen the chair next to the open window and considered closing it, but he hadn't wanted to make Pam feel as if he didn't trust her. He hadn't wanted to acknowledge his fear.

He held his head in his hands and began to weep. "I should have closed that window. If only I had closed it!"

"Don't blame yourself, Paul. It wasn't your fault. It would not have made any difference. We have enough shit to carry. You don't need to take this one on too," I said, hoping to alleviate his guilt.

He reached for his handkerchief and blew his nose. It was hard for him to go through the events so soon after her death. The grief came in waves that seemed to swallow him.

"I kissed her good-bye, reminding her that we were going to have dinner with some friends that evening. I told her that I would be home around six and that she should be ready."

I envied him for having kissed her good-bye.

"She was dressed for the day. She looked beautiful but sad. It made me sad to see her in her sundress, so sunless in her mood."

I asked him to describe what she had on. For some reason, I wanted to picture her in the last thing she wore. This was difficult for him.

"It doesn't matter. She changed before she jumped," he said.

"What do you mean?"

He told me that after he'd left for work, she went into the bedroom to ask Astrid how she looked. Astrid told her she looked beautiful. She had a hard time believing her and told Astrid that she didn't feel beautiful. She cried to Astrid about feeling as if all her self-worth had been stripped from her. She felt she had nothing to contribute to her family and to the world. She felt worthless. Astrid tried to reassure her that she had done so much with her young life, reminding her about all her accomplishments. It didn't seem to penetrate. Pam said she felt like a burden on her family, that she had nothing to give back. Astrid tried to console her, reassure her, and convince her that she was not a burden. She told her that we were all waiting for the day she could renew her commitment to her work and her life. She then kissed Astrid, thanked her for her support, and left the room.

This was the kiss I should have had. This was the kiss Astrid had told me about at the funeral.

He continued, "Astrid told me that Pam returned a few minutes later wearing another dress. She asked Astrid which one she liked better. Astrid told her that they both looked beautiful and it did not matter."

I waited for him to continue.

"I should have closed the window. Why didn't I close the window? Jesus! Had I only known!"

"Don't beat yourself up!" I said. "It wasn't your fault! I can argue that we never should have left for North Carolina. Perhaps if we had stayed, or at least one of us stayed, this might not have happened. We cannot make ourselves responsible for this act. We did the best we could do with the resources we had. It was out of our hands. It was her destiny."

It sounded good, but it didn't go down well with either of us. We both were despondent and despairing. I took his hand into mine. It felt right.

"What happened next?"

He explained that because he'd left for work earlier, Astrid filled him in on these details. She was alone with Pam. She told him that Pam had walked out of the room. It was close to 11:00 AM.

"The phone rang and Astrid answered it," he said.

His answering service had called regarding a patient. During Astrid's conversation with the answering service, Pam called to her, asking if she could use the phone. Astrid told her she was on the line with a patient and would be off in a few minutes.

When Astrid hung up just a few minutes later, she called to Pam to let her know that the phone was available. Pam did not respond. She took this to mean that Pam had left to pick up Dina.

A few minutes later, Dina called asking if Pam had left yet. She told Astrid that Pam was supposed to pick her up at 11:00. Astrid told Dina that she was probably on her way. She had no way of knowing that Pam had jumped off of the balcony.

About ten minutes later, there was a knock at the door. Not being able to get out of bed, Astrid was unable to open the door. The police were shouting and finally had to let themselves in by breaking the door jam. They came into the bedroom and asked who owned the apartment.

"She told them it belonged to me and that she was my girlfriend. She asked why they wanted to know."

He stopped, struggling to compose himself. I urged him to go on.

"They asked if I had a daughter about thirty years old or so. She told them that Pam was staying here for a few days. She was shocked when they told her a woman had jumped from the window of this apartment. They needed someone to identify the body. That's when she called me."

That was enough. I didn't need to know anymore.

6

A FEW WEEKS LATER

The time arrived to go through Pam's belongings. I knew this was going to be a difficult chore. We rummaged through with mixed emotions. We sometimes cried and laughed simultaneously.

The scattered arrangement of her dearest possessions revealed just how ill she was. Her clothes were disheveled. Her books and files were dumped into boxes. She collected junk, memorabilia, small notes, letters, and hundreds of legal pads with journals going back to high school. I felt like I was invading her privacy. I knew she would be angry had she known. I imagined that she knew.

She was a pack rat. She saved stuff that had no meaning at all. I found a letter I wrote to her about ten years previously. It surprised

me that she kept it. As I began reading, I flashed back to the visit
to England when I had written the letter.

Sam, my fourth husband, and I had been in England, visiting
his daughter and son-in-law, who lived in Hampstead, a suburb
of London. They had just had their first child. Martha was already
forty years old, and her husband, Marc, forty-four. Being a guest in
their historic, three-story, eighteenth century home, I was amazed
at all the changes in motherhood the nineties brought with it
compared to when I was a first-time mother.

Observing Marc and Martha together with their baby, I realized how inadequate Paul and I were as parents to Pam. I was
struck by the closeness and dedication the new parents provided
for their infant. Marc, a barrister, made it his business to be home
by five every day. He cherished his time with his firstborn child.
A simple gadget acting as a transmitter/receiver monitored the
baby's sounds from three stories above as we sipped tea in the
living room. This small, innocuous piece of plastic equipment on
the cocktail table kept us in constant communication with their
seven-pound baby boy. It registered every whimper, cry, kvetch,
grunt, gurgle, and breath coming from the crib in the nursery. I
envied them. They had the advantage of modern baby technology.
They had the advantage of being more mature, more financially
solvent, and more enlightened, which enabled them to provide a
support system for the mother and child. They were up-to-date

with the latest information on parenting. Because they were older
and more prepared for parenting than Paul and I were when we
had our first child, they were much more patient and relaxed in
their new roles.

They celebrated the Sabbath ritually each week with the baby
in Martha's arms so he would become accustomed to the family
tradition. Only one week old, he was already a participant by his
mere presence. I considered how barren my family life had been
and how rich theirs was. I tried to console myself by remembering
that we had celebrated the popular Jewish holidays.

In Martha and Marc's home, rearing children was different
from my experience, which made me realize what our children
needed that they didn't get. Martha refused to leave her baby to
go out for a meal or a movie, even though she had household help
and a nanny. Back in my early days of motherhood, I couldn't
wait to get out of the house. I went to a movie less than a week
after Pam was born. Rather than judge myself, I recognized how
limited and uninformed I was in so many important matters.
Obviously, motherhood manifests itself differently from woman
to woman. For some it doesn't necessarily come natural. Even if
it did, many distractions can make a vital difference. Hindsight is
easy. Nearly twenty-four years after my daughter Pam was born,
I started to realize how much closeness she was inadvertently
denied. This discovery had prompted me to write a twelve-page
letter to her. Contained within these reflections, I wrote all the
things I did not do that I wished I had done. I expressed my guilt

for any diminished attention, abandonment, neglect, or abuse I had somehow caused or perpetrated. I tried to make my amends and praised her for her accomplishments and achievements in spite of the inadequate parenting she received. I poured my heart out asking her for forgiveness in hopes it would mend our relationship, which always seemed to be fading in and out of estrangement. I assumed responsibility for failures or disappointments she experienced. I may have been self-deprecating, but I believed she needed some validation for her childhood perceptions. I naively assumed blame and responsibility as if I had the power to make or break her.

I didn't seal the envelope. It was as if I had a premonition.

That night I awoke in a state of terror from a nightmare. My nightgown was soaked with perspiration. I fled to the phone to call Pam, but before I dialed her number, I remembered that there was an eight or nine hour difference in time to LA, so I waited. By the time I called her, she was not at home, and by evening the dream and all the fear associated with it began to slip into my subconscious. I felt the need to share my dream with Pam, so I wrote it as a postscript the next morning before I mailed the letter.

The letter was long and rambling with what I perceived as too many apologies and affirmations for her accomplishments and successes. The last page had been torn in half and taped carefully to keep it intact. I had forgotten about the postscript. I looked at the damaged page and read it in shock.

P.S. I had a terrible dream about you last night. You came to me with a happy, "glowing" face. I was so happy to see you. When we embraced, you began to admonish me. Then you proceeded to jump off of a balcony, in clear view, onto the cement next to a fountain. People below screamed. I tried to rescue you. I ran screaming down the circling staircase, but by the time I got there it was too late. Your eyes were open and you were staring at me.

PART II

7

SHOCK AND GRIEF

S uicide is shocking. Losing a loved one to suicide is
insufferable. Losing a child is devastating, but losing a
child to suicide is beyond verbal description. No matter
what the circumstances, the survivor feels responsible. Guilt
plagued me. Days and night I tortured myself with thoughts
of what I could have done to prevent the suicide. There is no
consolation or reconciliation. I tried to come to grips that
Pam had an illness that had seized her mind, not unlike some
surrealistic, unrelenting, evil force.

I spent the first two months after Pam's death in emotional
shock. I was at first unaware that I had slipped into this state, even

though I had been told by the doctor in North Carolina the night I learned about her death. Those words had long been forgotten. Shock has a way of keeping you safe, not unlike the "shock" absorbers on a car. It's a defense mechanism to the reality of horror or something too painful to withstand. It almost seemed as if nothing had happened. I carried on as usual. I continued with my plans to take the sabbatical I had scheduled prior to her death. It seemed the right thing to do.

I returned to North Carolina, just after the shiva period ended, to the same cabin I had left the tragic morning after learning about Pam's death. Nothing had changed. The unpacked suitcases were exactly where I had left them. The bed was unmade. The bathroom light was still on. My toothbrush sat on its side on the sink and the showerhead was dripping. Time froze for me. I simply picked up where I had left off, as matter-of fact as if routinely coming home from work. My mind felt no pain. It seemed to be shrouded with a protective shield of bravado and inappropriate tranquility. I was happy to be in the mountains. My escape to the cool country air and change of atmosphere was all I wanted and needed.

Jim and I had talked about buying a house in the country where we would begin a new life. I combed the classifieds, searching for property. I had always wanted another home in Banner Elk, so I looked forward to the possibility of finding one now. Jim asked me to marry him. We had only known each other about six months and half that time we were not together. Jim was teaching and had not yet retired. He still lived in Wisconsin, and I lived in So.

Florida, so the time together had been very limited. The thought
of marriage was not appealing however. I was in such emotional
pain, that any escape was better than staying in reality. To say that
I was numbed out, was putting it mildly.

It didn't take long before I came across exactly what I wanted:
a twenty-one acre estate with a lovely three-bedroom cottage set
high on a hill overlooking a red barn, a babbling brook, a fifty-
mile view, and all in the center of the Pisgah National Forest, with
the most majestic sunsets imaginable. How could I go wrong? I
submitted a much lower bid than the asking price, and, much to
my surprise, the seller accepted. I was ecstatic. I wrote a deposit
check and began singing, "Nothing could be finer than to be in
Carolina in the morning." Jim and I set a closing for October 30
and a wedding date for December 24. All I could think about was
the changes I would make in the house, and how I would live there
with Jim happily ever after. I contacted an architect and contractor
to draw up plans and prepare cost estimates. I never once considered
I was suffering from the shock of losing my daughter.

By the end of July, I began to emerge from my emotional stupor
and realized that I must be out of my mind. Not only did I not
want to move to North Carolina, which would have meant giving up my Florida practice and moving away from my family, the
remaining vestige of my sanity, but I was also convinced that I was
not in love with Jim and that I had nothing to offer any relationship while my heart was filled with grief. I had made some life
decisions while I was in the thick of grief, loss, and shock and was

out of touch with my true feelings. Another "me" was doing this. This other me (my bravado self) had taken over and made these untimely and preposterous decisions that ultimately cost me the loss of the property, the $10,000 deposit, and countless hours of sleep on top of the grief I was already suffering.

Driving back to Miami from North Carolina without Jim (he returned home to resume his job), I reconciled that I would not marry him. I became in touch with the pressure I felt that was buried beneath the shock. Jim called it "support," but, in truth, it was a form of control, and it began to feel more like oppression. At last, my brain had fully awakened and I had to face the truth. I was not ready for marriage or a house in North Carolina or any other unnecessary distractions.

In spite of all these disturbing feelings, I decided to continue my sabbatical, fly to Santa Fe for a pre-scheduled conference, and be with Jim until the end of August as originally planned, even though I knew the outcome. So now I had a new feeling to add to my emotional parfait—a nagging, persistent fear that told me the decision to marry Jim was wrong. Don't do it! I was out of sorts the entire two weeks I was with Jim. I was in turmoil, fluctuating between guilt and grief. An impending doom filled me, and I knew if I didn't heed its warning I would suffer serious regrets. Upon returning home, I told Jim how I felt and that I wanted out. He became enraged, which demonstrated obsession and an unwilling- ness to let go. We began a tortuous journey of maybes and useless attempts at reconciliation that ultimately ended in breakup.

I learned a crucial lesson: <u>one should never ever make life deci</u>-<u>sions while in shock, grief, or mourning. Feelings cannot be trusted,</u> <u>and they are most often distorted by shock. Trust your body.</u> It generally speaks the truth. The entire event with Jim was disastrous and undeniably a difficult experience in my life.

Once I realized that I would not be able to conclude the acquisition of the house, I tried desperately to salvage the $10,000 contract deposit. I couldn't afford the amount due on closing. Then the stock market plunged that August. I searched desperately for options. I had some friends who were looking for a second home in the mountains, so I shared with them what had happened, hoping one of them might be interested in taking over the contract. By the time I was able to find a couple who eventually bought the house (for far more than I had offered), the closing date had passed and the seller was unwilling to return my deposit.

The seller had recently undergone a successful heart transplant. I wrote him a letter explaining that I had been in a state of shock when I made the offer. My daughter had been dead only two weeks and I had made a mistake. I also reminded him that I had found him a new buyer for a much larger sum and wondered if he could find it in his "new heart" to return my deposit. My naiveté and hope was replaced by disappointment and anger when he refused to consider my request. This was yet another hard lesson to digest.

When I returned home from my sabbatical in September, I thought it wise to participate in a support group for mourners. I joined a local grief-counseling group that met twice a month. I had not yet sought private counseling, believing that I could deal with Pam's death without outside help. I knew all about grief and thought I had the professional experience to handle my own.

I entered the room where a dozen or so bereaved parents and spouses milled about. These were all suicide survivors, as they were called, those having lost loved ones by suicide. Inwardly I balked. I didn't want to be labeled a "suicide survivor." I felt different and out of place, but I took my seat between two other parents who shared a common denominator of losing their adult child through suicide. Some members had attended for years. I was appalled. How could anyone keep coming to a grief group for such a prolonged period of time? Not me. I am not going to make a mission out of this loss, and I am not going to martyr myself in self-pity and reliance on emotional crutches. I sat there bewildered and angered that I was an attendee. I didn't feel that I needed or wanted to be a part of this grieving group. I still was not in touch with my grief.

I listened to the stories they told while tears streamed down their faces. Some were unable to look up, while others buried their faces in their hands. Why was I not crying? Why was I feeling detached? Was there something wrong with me? I kept looking at my watch, waiting impatiently for the time to pass. As I heard their stories, I kept playing in my mind my own imaginary video of Pam's death. No tears came when I related my story. It was as if I were an automaton relaying my story.

As the weeks of attendance passed, I began to take on the role of the co-therapist in the group, as if all the participants were my patients. I forgot that it was I who had come for help. I volunteered to lead the group when the leader was absent, but she declined my offer. I was miffed. I thought I was a better counselor than she. She had no credentials and I had been a seasoned therapist for many years. She gently reminded me that I was still too fresh from my experience to lead a group. I didn't agree. Feeling unappreciated and annoyed, I discontinued attending.

I began writing this book as a catharsis—a mechanism whereby I might vent my feelings and emotions. The evening I began writing was the night before I was to begin a "Five Day Intensive," a forty-hour therapy program. I designed this "intensive" to work with clients who lived away from South Florida and wanted to do Original Pain Therapy (OPT). I had scheduled this months before Pam's death, so I felt slightly intimidated, fearing that under the circumstances I would not be able to do my best. The client flew in from another state, anxiously awaiting an opportunity for exploration, growth, and change. She had no knowledge of my loss. I had to fulfill my commitment only two months after my daughter had been tragically plucked from life. Yet, aware of my professional responsibility and need for a decent night's sleep, I felt compelled to sit at my computer and write.

Nights like this are common. Grievers become nocturnal. Fears usually are omnipresent. I became used to them. I knew that when the sun surfaced over the blue Atlantic outside my window, the fears would go to sleep like a vampire that surreptitiously sneaks into its coffin just before the sun rises, only to return again the next night. My fears were my companions. They became familiar, almost like old friends.

I lived alone. My other children were grown and had been living on their own for quite a while. I had no pets, because the condominium association did not allow them. It would probably have helped to have a pet, something to be responsible for and by which to feel needed—a reminder that life goes on and we need to make the best of it.

The nights were lonely, oftentimes scary. But there was something friendly and familiar about them too. They seemed to engender creativity. Perhaps it was the silence and lack of distractions that made it easier to focus. Sometimes it wasn't. Perhaps my angel came, called me to the computer, and whispered to my unconscious, "Write, Mother, just write." Whatever it was, it felt comforting. It felt as if I was writing through Pam.

The tension I carried gripped me like a vice. I began to experience chronic pain in my neck as well as my cervical and lumbar spine. I thought the chronic dull pain in my chest might be heartache. Perhaps it was anxiety or phantom pains of what used to be and is no longer. Sometimes I had no voice, only the sorrow where my voice once lived. I had two pinched nerves, and the doctor diagnosed multiple degenerative disc disease and stenosis of the spine. I began bleeding two years after menopause. Maybe I would have had the stenosis and bleeding anyway. I don't know. I didn't take any medications. Perhaps I should have. I preferred to feel the pain. I believed it expedited the prevailing grief process.

I came into full-blown grief! I felt tired, fatigued, and lethargic most of the day. I needed to sleep a lot. There were days when I fell asleep on the couch, losing touch with time. It was an effort to even think. And when I did, my thoughts were filled only with Pam. There wasn't a moment she left my mind. I left no room in my brain for any other thoughts. Making decisions was nearly impossible. I felt like I had been swallowed into a vacuum or had fallen down some rabbit hole like Alice in Wonderland. The world looked different. The colors were gone. Life felt meaningless and empty. Nothing seemed to matter or make any difference. I had sight, but I didn't see. I heard, but it was so difficult to listen. The music was gone. I couldn't hear the birds. I couldn't see the trees, and I couldn't feel any joy.

I felt better when I forced myself to take long walks and have conversations with my angel. I asked her over and over again, "Why, Pam? Why did you do it?" I heard her voice inside my head continuing to comfort me with the same refrain. "I didn't do it, Mom. I was called. I am at peace. I am home. Please know that I will never leave you. I am with you all the time." It was the same conversation we'd had in the shower the first night of shiva. I wondered if I'd really heard those words or imagined them.

Occasionally I screamed at her. "How could you? How could you do this to us? Bitch, you bitch!" I would shout, as if she was there. But then it came again, her voice inside my head, reassuring me that she'd had no choice, begging me to understand and forgive her. I sighed, and said with a heart so heavy it was almost impossible to breathe, "I forgive you. I forgive you. I love you, no matter!"

I harbored so much anger that it felt only natural to cast the blame anywhere and everywhere—particularly at myself. I wanted to blame her father. I began to find fault in everything he ever did or didn't do. I held him responsible for not closing the window when he noticed it open. After all, I wondered, Where was he? What was he thinking? I blamed him for not realizing how ill she really was. I attacked him in my thoughts for not being able to do something. He was her father, a physician, and a man with connections for anything. He could get great seats at any of the sports games, tickets to Broadway theaters, and seating at Joe's Stone Crabs in ten minutes, yet he couldn't save his daughter. I'd left her alone with him for the very first time so I could go away on my sabbatical. After being Pam's guardians for the last few months, my other daughters needed a break. We all desperately needed a break. All Paul had to do was to be aware, be present, attuned, and be alert to her facial expressions, her moods, and her behavior. He needed to listen and watch for signs. He needed to do something that required more than just paying the bills.

Along with this anger aimed at Paul, I recalled his abandonment I had felt during our marriage—the nights I had slept alone because there was some casino or racetrack that had held more interest for him than our children or me. Suddenly, I hated him for his addiction, for his obsessive-compulsive behaviors, and for his lack of participation in our lives when the children were little.

I hated him for not hearing me when I tried to tell him how seriously ill Pam was and for denying that I had told him how ill she was. I cringed even having to look at him. He reminded me of his mistakes. He reminded me of mine. I cursed him in the night, screaming obscenities laced with tears and interminable pain. I was glad he was not there. He didn't need to hear my wrath. But truth be told, it was neither his fault nor mine.

I contemplated suing the doctors, the hospitals, the insurance company, and anyone who had ever seen her and not made the correct diagnosis and professional judgment to institutionalize her. I hated the whole mental health system. I believed the doctors and therapists were all culpable and had acted irresponsibly. In my heartache and fears I lashed out at them, labeling them quacks and incompetents, disinterested, detached, and dissociated. I hated the stoic, stone-faced look on their faces when I shared my pain and concern. I wondered if they ever gave Pam a moment's thought after their sessions were over. I wondered if they ever thought about Pam and her illness when they were on the golf course, on their fishing boats, at a Dolphins game, or in their beds at night. I wondered if they had one conscious thought of her.

I knew that mental health professionals are trained to deal with transference and counter-transference, to separate our feelings from those of our clients. I knew that it is not productive to carry patients' problems home with us. I also knew that some of those well-trained, intellectual, robotic, left-brain creatures possessed real feelings, who did carry home stuff that should have been left at the office, who probably had more than a few sleepless nights worrying about a patient. I knew because I was not the only one who did this.

I wondered how many people had fallen through the cracks in the same system that had failed my daughter. The health profession, in particular the health mental system, became the target of my silent rage. They became the murderers, the executioners, and the sons of bitches who never gave a damn. They all hid behind their empty words, "I did the best I could," or "She just doesn't meet the criteria for hospitalization." I hated those words.

If only I had let Pam come with her sisters. If only I had insisted that her psychiatrist hospitalize her when I had spoken to her earlier. If only Pam had not missed her appointment with her psychiatrist. If only I had been more indulgent, more sympathetic, more understanding, and patient.

Two days after arriving home from Santa Fe, I returned a call from Pam's last psychiatrist, an orthodox Jewish woman in her early forties and a mother of young children. She asked me to come in for any closure I might need. I felt compelled to do so because I needed to vent my anger, though I figured she would likely use that supercilious phrase "I did the best I could do." I knew she wasn't God, and, in fact, she had probably done her best.

I sat there on the same sofa where only a few weeks earlier Pam and I had sat together. I had come during her session so her psychiatrist would hear my concerns. I wanted no stone left unturned. I'd suggested she prescribe another antipsychotic drug that Pam had not used before. She had said that she wanted to wait a while to see how the one she was giving her was working. I had tried with all my professional and maternal efforts to convince her that it was not working and that another drug should be considered. I'd even suggested the drug as well as the use of electric shock therapy. She had remained adamant, reminding me in her polite, professional voice that she was the doctor and would, of course, make those decisions.

Now weeks later, I just listened as she rambled on and on about her choices and my interpretations. I noticed she was fidgeting and crying. I offered her one of her own tissues. I never reached for one myself. It struck me that I was like the psychiatrist and she, the patient. I revealed no feelings, only rhetoric. I was stoic and detached. I was stronger than her. I imagine that she'd had some sleepless nights, too.

Back in the privacy of my apartment I loaded my guilt gun every night, aimed it toward my heart, and pulled the trigger until my soul bled to death. I felt I deserved to die. I, her mother, accomplished therapist, healer of others, author, speaker, blah, blah, blah—I had let her die. I knew in my heart she was sick. I knew in my mind she may die. What was I thinking? Where was I? Why didn't I do something to prevent this atrocity? Why? Why? Why? I blamed myself for everything. I started with the first time I'd rocked the carriage too hard when she was only two months old and was ceaselessly crying. I followed the timeline through our history to our last conversation when I had asked her if she thought about suicide. My whole life as a mother flashed by me with only the mistakes on the film. I knew if I continued this perpetual self-flagellation, I would be sick, too. I had to break the shame spiral, but I didn't know how.

Hardly anyone noticed my pain. I lived alone, and when I was with my other children, I managed to control these feelings. I went to work every day. It felt like hell, a darkness from which I would never return. I went through the motions. The days were a jumble. Monday felt like Friday or Wednesday. I had to earn a living to support myself, so I could not afford to get sick.

I helped my clients. They saw me struggling yet functioning with this worst possible experience anyone can ever face. My clients told me that their problems seemed pale compared to mine. They saw my strength, which I did not. They saw my weakness and vulnerability that I made no effort to disguise. Sometimes I cried in front of them, something therapists have been trained not to do. But my clients didn't seem to mind. It helped them realize that we are all vulnerable. They learned that no one is spared pain and problems, that grieving is inevitable. They learned that adversity could breed new strength. They learned that anger is okay, that feeling responsible and guilty is part of the grief process. They learned that crying is healing, that unless one experiences the pain and sorrow, letting go is not possible.

Grief is a process with stages. First comes the shock and denial. Shock is followed by anger and fear. You're angry with the deceased, then you're angry with yourself and sometimes your partner. Then the anger spreads everywhere and becomes pervasive. Then the anger changes to sadness and a deep sense of loss. Finally comes acceptance, which makes it possible to forgive—forgive God, forgive my child, and forgive myself for all the "what ifs" and all the things I didn't or did do. Forgiveness enables letting go. For me it was letting go of the grandchildren Pam might have blessed me with, letting go of the hopes that she would recover and lead a full life, letting go of the thoughts of what I should have done differently, even though I did everything I could have done. From this process, a gradual peace paves the way for a better tomorrow. We can't accept or forgive until we acknowledge all the stages: denial, anger, fear, sadness, and loss. It's not easy. It's not possible to do it alone. Other people are necessary to validate the experience and to support the reality. That is why I went to a grief counselor to help me deal with the pain and loss. I had not yet been willing to relinquish my denial, so I abandoned the therapy. It was months before I was ready to grieve fully. Everyone has their own timetable. Each of us grieves in our own way and in our own time.

I have learned what really is important in life and what really matters: control is an illusion; money is necessary, but not as important as I once thought; family and friends are very important; love is most important, for love heals.

I was gratified that I could allow my clients to observe this process as I experienced it. Now I can say that I truly comprehend the experience of grief and mourning. I have, in fact, lived life more fully as a consequence of having gone through it myself. I am a better therapist. I have more compassion and empathy for others who suffer loss and grief. I am a kindred spirit to their experiences. My adversity made me stronger and gave me a fierce sense of empowerment. I am able to cope better with the stresses of life. I understand more about "letting go." I realize that nothing is forever and that life has no guarantees. I live life in the moment, for nothing is forever.

8

PAM: THE WOMAN, THE THERAPIST, THE PATIENT

There was little separation between Pam the therapist and Pam the ill woman, and yet each was distinctive at times. In the beginning of her illness, the symptoms were hardly recognizable. When the disease grabbed hold, it ran riot in her.

I am not sure when her illness first began. Most likely it was always there, but not always visible. Perhaps I didn't want to see it, or it was too subtle to notice.

Her development was tumultuous with a jumble of hostile and loving behaviors. As I mentioned earlier, as an infant and toddler, Pam demonstrated extreme behaviors, which I didn't discern as abnormal because I'd never had a child before and didn't have a point of reference.

It was difficult to grasp who she really was. It was as if there were two of her, the good child and the bad. Everyone said she would outgrow it. She did, but something else always replaced it that was just as bad or even worse. As a child, she wore a perpetual smile. Her laughter filled the house. She was beautiful, perhaps more beautiful than any child I had ever seen. Too beautiful to be mine, I often thought.

We adored her. Her father worshipped her. From birth, he called her Rosanna Podesta, the actress who had played Helen in the 1956 film *Helen of Troy*. As time passed, she grew more beautiful.

She was twenty-one months old when my next child, Monica, was born. Pam embraced her wholeheartedly. There didn't seem to be a jealous bone in her body. She genuinely loved being the older sister caring for the baby and making her feel welcome. As the other children arrived, all within seven years of one another, she seemed to take on the role of caregiver and mentor. In fact, my other children would say that she molded their lives. Later on, Pam became their surrogate mother. When I divorced Paul after thirteen rocky years of marriage, times were tough, tougher than I ever imagined. I didn't know how we would survive. Although the courts awarded me the large house in the "gilded ghetto" and provided me with some child support and limited alimony, there wasn't enough money to support the upkeep of our home. Paul soon left the state for a job in the Midwest. I used the alimony to pay tuition to earn my master's degree in social work in anticipation of earning more to be able to support my family.

Only eleven years old, Pam took over. She became the "little mother" during my frequent absences while I was attending graduate school. She tried in her limited way to be there for the other children. She helped dress them in the morning, prepared their breakfasts, sent them off to school with their lunches, and walked them safely across the street to the schoolyard. All but Aaron went to the same elementary school: Pam was in the sixth grade, Monica was in the fourth, Todd in the second, Erika in kindergarten. Aaron attended nursery school. Pam waited until the bus came for Aaron before she went to school. The demands and stress were unbearable for her to take on so soon. I worried about this but didn't have much choice.

By the time Pam turned sixteen, she was frequently mistaken for Brooke Shields. Popular, talented, and intelligent, she was a cheerleader in high school and looked like a teenage movie star. I had been married nearly four years to Dennis. Pam's father was practicing medicine in a rural town in Missouri. This was when she was acting out what I thought was normal adolescent rebellion. But like most of her behavior, it seemed to go a little further than the other teenagers. She was angry with me for divorcing her father, whom she had always idealized. He was her beloved Daddy, and I was the wicked woman who'd sent him away. He was the good parent; I was the bad one. Sometimes she idealized me and other times she raged against me with out-of-control fury. She was angry about my marriage to Dennis. Pam was enraged that he attempted to take her father's place and acted as spokesperson on behalf of the other children, who also resented him.

During her growing-up years, a series of events and interactions should have alerted me to the onset of Pam's mental illness. But as it is with so many parents, we are oftentimes the last to recognize the signals and the first to deny them. For a long time, I resisted acknowledging what was happening, until finally I could no longer deny the seriousness of her condition.

As far back as I can remember, she was always sloppy. Her desk was messy. Her room and drawers were messy with dirty clothes tossed onto clean ones, and her closet looked like it had been hit by a tornado—the hangers were empty except for the few that were used as rods to drape clothes on. Traces of food and wrappers lay scattered on the floor, under the bed, in the closet—everywhere they weren't supposed to be. She had to be reminded daily to shower, to wash her hair, brush her teeth, shave her legs and underarms, and use deodorant. Her personal hygiene was atrocious. In the depth of her illness, she refused to use sanitary napkins or Tampax during her menstruation. She was unkempt, untidy, disheveled, and unconcerned about her personal belongings. Everyone thought that she was spoiled and that she expected others to pick up after her. We tried every way we knew to break these bad habits. No matter how often I disciplined her on this, she never changed. She could not tolerate my attempts at confrontation and discipline.

I gave her a "Sweet 16" birthday party. After all of her friends had gone home, we had sat together on the living room floor. With tears of joy, she declared her love and devotion to me, thanking me for being the "best Mom in the world" and for hosting the celebration for her sixteenth birthday. Twenty-five days later she repeated the same words on my fortieth birthday. One month later, just before Thanksgiving, she decided to leave me and live with her father. It was hard for me to believe and accept that she was gone. I was devastated. She had chosen to leave her high school friends, her sisters, brothers, and her grandparents to travel to an unknown place far away so she could join her father and become what appeared to be his "surrogate wife." She needed to hurt me, which she did, a hurt I will never forget. She needed to rescue him, and so she left all of us behind. There was nothing I could do or say that would sway her. No matter how I cried or pleaded, I could not influence her decision. Her friends tried to dissuade her. Her family tried. Nothing worked. It felt as though I lost her to a whim.

I was heartbroken. I yearned for her and would lie awake nights wondering if she missed me. I doubted my parenting skills and berated myself for not doing a better job. I felt culpable for what had happened. These were the times I regretted divorcing Paul. I blamed my failure as a mother. I blamed myself that there was neither a mother nor a father at home for my children. I blamed Paul and his lack of responsibility in our lives. I needed to find a reason why this was happening.

I lived three miles from my office. I walked there each day with a pain in my heart so heavy that I thought I would implode. I tried desperately to discharge my pain and grief. As if talking to Pam, I spoke into a small tape recorder as I walked each morning, describing each landmark in our lives. I sang the songs we sang together and rehashed the events of the previous days, filling the tape by the time I reached my office, and hoping to jar her nostalgia as a reminder of "home." I sent her the tapes and knew she would recognize the love I held in my heart. I hoped she would hear my sorrow and tell me she wanted to come home. But that could happen only on her terms.

She finally returned right before her senior year of high school. By then Dennis was out and Jerry was in. That never sat well with her. Pam's father was her knight in shining armor. She was his princess. She lived out all his wishes and assignments. She would tell me that he "glamorized" her, that he made her feel like a trophy daughter, which contaminated her role and their relationship. He would send her a dozen roses for birthdays, illnesses, special events, and sometimes for no reason at all. She disclosed to me much later that she felt more like his surrogate lover than a daughter.

Although there had never been any overt sexual abuse, she often felt confused about her identity with him. They idealized each other. He was her hero, her champion, and the love of her life. When she later went into therapy, she was able to sort out her identity with him. But she'd internalized so much of his unresolved pain and sorrow that she often didn't know where he ended and she began.

They were more than bonded. They were enmeshed. It was risky business. She needed him and he needed her. Her illness fostered her dependency, and although he complained, he also enabled it. It was his way of showing his love for her. This was likely why he found it difficult to believe she was sick. We simply didn't comprehend. Neither did most others, including some of her therapists and psychiatrists.

Bipolar disorder is illusive. It is episodic, unpredictable, and inconsistent. It can be misdiagnosed because it mimics so many other psychiatric disorders. It can coexist with a variety of other possible mental diagnoses. Because of the comorbidity, it can fool the best of minds, and it did in Pam's case. Her illness had already shown itself, but we were too close to it and unable to recognize it as a mental disorder. I thought she was acting out, behaving like a spoiled brat. And perhaps she was. But now that I look back, I see the signs were there, only I couldn't recognize them.

In her book *His Bright Light*, Danielle Steele describes her son as "outrageous." This was not unlike Pam. Her aggression was often spontaneous and autonomous. It shot out like a rocket. She was easily triggered into explosive fits that were so opposite from her seemingly gentle nature. Her impulsive behavior in certain instances terrified me. Soon after she completed her master's degree at Adelphi College, I went to visit her in New York. One afternoon we drove down Third Avenue into Manhattan. I was in the passenger seat. A truck that had been tailing too closely behind lightly bumped the car. Both Pam and the truck driver pulled over to a side street, where she proceeded to confront him face-to-face with a wrath that terrified me. She verbally attacked him without reserve, poking her index finger under his chin, shouting, "Don't fuck with me!" It startled me. How could she take such a chance? He could have easily been triggered by such an inappropriate assault. But he backed off, likely fearing she was out of control or crazy. I admonished her later, cautioning her about the risk she took and asking her to think of the consequences before she acted so aggressively. She possessed no sense of caution. She was fearless.

In yet another incident a few years later, her father, Astrid, all five of our grown children, and I were having dinner together in a restaurant in Florida. Without provocation, she suddenly became aggressive toward me. She erupted into a verbal assault for no apparent cause and proceeded to wage war on me, attacking every aspect of my character and motherhood. She showed no restraint or concern for anyone in the restaurant. The family became intimidated by her sudden outburst and vilification of me. Unable to calm her, I chose to leave.

Pam was a paradox. She seemed to possess an abundance of courage and yet a naiveté and innocence that was disarming and almost childlike. She often called herself "Pami Annie Daisy." This was the name she gave to her inner child. At the center, she would often dress in costume, like a little girl when she wanted to be in the role of her inner child. Her clients enjoyed her playfulness, which encouraged them to engage with their own inner child.

When meeting children, she always engaged with them at their own level. She was like a Pied Piper.

Pam always radiated an energy that attracted people. Her sorority sister once told me that when Pam entered a room, the charge was so great that everyone stopped what they were doing. Her essence was magnetic, charismatic. She drew people to her. From early on, her charm and beauty were her hallmark. She had a chutzpa (nerve) about her that startled people. Her allure neutralized any negative response others might have had to her precocity. We assumed she was gregarious, which we considered a positive behavior; however, as she grew into adulthood, it bordered on bizarre and at times inappropriate.

On one occasion, she and her fiancé Josef were having lunch in New York with Paul and me at Rockefeller Plaza when she battled with the waiter. She'd ordered a Monterey Jack cheese omelet, and when the waiter served it, she became enraged because she was convinced the cheese was not Monterey Jack. He offered to exchange it for another item, but she adamantly refused, insisting he bring back another omelet with the correct cheese. Feeling uncomfortable and embarrassed by the scene she'd made, her father and I tried to persuade her to select something else from the menu. The waiter brought her another omelet, again to her dissatisfaction. She then demanded to see the chef and proceeded to the kitchen to confront him about the misrepresentation, declaring that she knew what Monterey Jack cheese looked and tasted like and that was not the cheese in the omelet. She refused anything else to eat. I was stunned and humiliated. She walked on the edge of eccentricity.

These types of incidents occurred intermittently but became more and more frequent as the disease progressed. We did not suspect that her erratic mood swings, sloppiness, and inability to contain herself were indicative of a psychiatric disorder. We were dumbfounded because in between these occasions she acted responsibly and kindheartedly. We were clueless that a mental illness was weaving its way inside her brain, slowly taking over her mind and her spirit. We all slipped into the natural denial. But denial is funny stuff. We rationalize to minimize what we fear is the truth. Rationalization usually wins out because we really don't want to believe the truth. The truth is too painful.

Somehow Pam managed to manage. She always had this uncanny ability to fake life. To the world she looked together. She had a busy practice but never seemed to have any money. I never really understood why. After her death, her friends told me that no matter how much she earned, she was always in debt. She spent impulsively and frivolously, over-indulging herself and her friends. She made extensive, long distance phone calls without concern for the cost. She traveled at whim and maxed out her credit cards. As with the three-carat pear-shaped engagement ring I had given her, things disappeared without her knowing where they went. She ignored tickets for traffic violations. She stuffed them in the glove compartment in her car and forgot about them. If she didn't see them, then in her disturbed mind, they weren't there. She would ignore her bills until creditors threatened to turn off the electricity or telephone. Her credit rating was so poor that she was unable to obtain a loan for a car. She never saw herself as culpable. She always had an excuse, usually blaming others for her problems. She copped an attitude with a sense of omnipotence, as if she was above the law. The rules didn't apply to her. She tried to sweep everything under the carpet, but her wreckage always caught up with her.

Pam seemed always to live in and for the moment, giving herself permission to be free-spirited, self-indulgent, and unbridled. She lacked propriety and responsibility. And yet, there were times she was so self-righteous and virtuous as if to overcompensate and cover up for her mistakes and the times she acted inappropriately or wrongful. It was her way of righting the wrong and absolving the guilt that she seemed to hide and seldom shared with us. Her acting out was oftentimes dangerous to her well-being.

The extremes in her behavior matched her mood swings. I never knew what to expect. Her anxiety could peak to panic attacks. Her depression could descend to near madness. Her jubilance, serenity, and goodwill were equally out of proportion. She was often too loud, too extravagant, and too reckless. She applied her makeup on improperly cleaned skin and without any effort or care so that it looked slopped on. Her clothes were never completely clean or pressed. They were often soiled, ill-fitting, too tight, too short, or unbecoming. She never seemed to notice or care about her appearance. She acted promiscuous at times, and then at others as if she lived in a convent.

She was a master of smoke and mirrors. There were times she looked positively, breathtakingly beautiful. She could leave an audience spellbound with her speaking ability, mesmerizing them with her knowledge and presentation. She carried it all off like a pro until the disease took over.

For the most part she was kind and caring, warm and wonderful, loving and compassionate, tender and sensitive, sweet and incredibly intelligent. She was a great listener, an incomparably gifted therapist, and exemplary friend. Anyone she befriended loved her unconditionally and forever. They always gave her the benefit of the doubt and forgiveness whenever she caused an altercation, because she gave so much of herself and asked for so little in return.

Our relationship was as rocky as her illness. It yawed between extremes of love and compassion, and then shifted to the other with vengeance and hostility. She was topsy-turvy and chaotic, confusing everyone who knew her, including me.

She felt safe with me. She discharged her anger at me contemptuously. Although I challenged her behavior, she knew I would never abandon her. It was easier to express her feelings to her mother. She and I had a different relationship from the one she had with her father. Different from the one she had with her siblings, other family members, and friends. Additionally, we shared the same profession.

Once when we were together in North Carolina facilitating group therapy, she became enraged with me. She had been trying to understand her feelings of insecurity. She was defending her fear, using anger as a club. When she was able to identify and acknowledge her feelings as fear, she revealed that she was afraid she would never be as good as me. I was shocked. I thought her to be the more gifted therapist, in spite of her youth and lack of life experience. The competition she felt was so surprising and so well concealed that I never knew it existed.

In retrospect, the signs were always there. We just didn't know about this illness. It was lurking in her childhood, following her like a shadow, slowly, steadfastly. It surreptitiously invaded her mind, took over her brain, wrestled with her reasoning until it fractured her spirit and took her from us. This was the nature of her bipolar I disorder. She would often say that she felt possessed. As time progressed, her symptoms began to manifest into more hallucinations as grandiose and persecutory delusions.

One evening after we did a radio performance in Asheville, North Carolina, and were driving to our cabin in Banner Elk, she suddenly screamed out, "Mom! Watch out!"

"What's wrong?" I said startled at her sudden burst of emotion.

"Out there!" she said, pointing to the windshield. "Out there!"

"What? What's out there?" I asked, puzzled because I saw nothing but the open road before us.

"It's your inner child! Be careful! You're going to run her over!"

I was stunned. She hallucinated what she perceived to be my inner child. Frantic, I pulled over to the side of the road. She was nearly hysterical, sobbing that I'd almost killed my inner child. It took some time to settle her down, and then she said that she had been having intrusive thoughts that would without warning invade her mind, leading her to believe that what she experienced was real. I had a difficult time convincing her that there was no child in the road and that perhaps she needed to see a psychiatrist for medication management. Perhaps she needed an antipsychotic. We drove on to Banner Elk where we held a retreat. She did not share another hallucination until the last two years of her life.

Pam started on medication but frequently discontinued it without our knowledge. As her illness progressed and we spent more time with her, we were able to see her delusional psychosis spill out in spite of her effort to contain it. It became impossible for her to camouflage it all the time. Even though she had lucid moments, her flight of ideas, racing thoughts, ideas of reference and paranoia broke through any attempt to disguise it. She would attach significance to symbols, words, and numbers as if they were sending her coded messages that only she could interpret.

One instance while she was living with her sisters, she became paranoid over a minor incident. The mail came in with the wrong date, most probably a typo. She interpreted this to mean that there was a conspiracy with the government against her. Erika tried to reason with her to no avail. She had fantasies about the Devil and of good and evil, where she was being chosen to be the mediator between God and Lucifer. Her hallucinations were hard to repress. Movies like *L.A. Story* with Steve Martin and *The Devil's Advocate* with Al Pacino would send her into a panic, triggering paranoia and fears. *L.A. Story* reflected images of "signs" and the ability to gain deeper meaning in the signs. This idea of reference was part of her illness, driving her to find special personal significance in something totally unrelated. She had been seeing signs for years but never revealed her interpretations and meanings to me. The move to Florida amplified them. She lost the ability to distinguish between reality and fantasy. She absorbed anything that was cryptic or surreal. This was when we knew she did not take her medication, even though she swore she had.

Part of her delusion was her fear that the Devil was determined to take her soul, and the medicine would make her more vulnerable to his command. Her only real hope, the medicine, to her had been contaminated by her delusions. Even more disconcerting was that when she took the medicine, she appeared to fall into a semi-stupor. She could barely stay alert, think clearly, or function, despite adjustments in both drugs and dosages. It seemed she was damned if she did and damned if she didn't. She hated having racing psychotic thoughts and feeling drugged. This contributed to her resistance to staying on the medication. Finally, her delusions made the decision for her.

9

THE
QUINTESSENTIAL
THERAPIST
DOOMED

P am began her own personal therapy from the time
she attended her freshman year at the University of
Missouri. She seemed to recognize her problems and
the need for professional help. She continued her therapy
all throughout the years she was away. After she returned to
South Florida, just three years before her death, she saw several
therapists and at least five psychiatrists. Her life was woven
with therapy. Perhaps her unconscious motivation to become
a therapist was to heal her own wounds.

The John Bradshaw Center in LA had helped launch Pam's career, and she continued much of the work she was trained to do there. She traveled to North Carolina and Florida to work with me at the retreats I provided for my clients, and together we helped transform many lives. Both of us had been trained by the center and we were an effective team, helping our clients work through pain and reach heights of awareness they never thought possible. We gave seminars, workshops, and facilitated retreats together. Our bonding transcended our relationship. We were colleagues. We were friends. We were each other's mentor.

As a therapist, Pam excelled. Her patients trusted her. They would expose themselves fully to her. There were no limits or restraints. She possessed the wonder and curiosity of a child, while at the same time a grandiosity and arrogance that would leap out like a wild animal attacking its prey. She drew the lightening to herself, instigating and antagonizing her clients to bring out their dark sides. Hers met theirs. I watched her during treatment sessions. She was bold, baiting a subject until he or she leaped at her, reacting with their repressed aggression. She drew out their venom, their rage, and then she embraced them with a love they had never experienced. She embraced their shadow side and taught them to do the same. She gave them permission to feel their shameful feelings. She taught them to love themselves. She changed the colors of their minds. She was a born healer and this was her mission. I would watch in awe. She was talented. But deep inside I questioned her motives and her fearlessness as she manipulated the therapy to draw blood like a matador. How could she be so nonchalant about the process, I would often wonder. Where is her fear? Why is she so complacent?

"Aren't you afraid?" I asked more than once.

"You can take your patients only as far as you've gone yourself. Anger doesn't intimidate me. I have seen my own," was her typical response.

Her reply made me nervous. I'd worked with anger with many of my clients. But there were boundaries and cautions that I respected. Pam applied the same technique to everyone, even those patients who didn't need to discharge rage. I wondered where her boundaries were. She helped her clients create them, yet hers were evanescent. I wondered if she might absorb and assimilate the negative energies she so effectively drained from her patients, similar as what occurs during exorcism. However, she had no way to discharge the energy. It gathered inside her until it threatened to blow. She extracted the psychological poison from them but had no way of releasing it herself. When one absorbs the toxic energy and shame of another human being to the point of saturation—like the prisoner in *The Green Mile* who was able to spew the toxic energy he absorbed from other inmates—releasing the energy is essential to one's sanity. Without boundaries, implosion is inevitable. Mother Teresa understood this. She allowed her staff to work only four hours at a time, then required them to rest.

Pam's patients always came first, to the exclusion of herself. She was a tireless worker. When she was lucid, the life changes she enabled in her patients were remarkable. She seemed to know exactly what they needed. Her empathic nature restored their long-lost trust. She carefully measured their ability to cope with the work. She gauged them for resistance. She calculated their ego strengths. She understood and respected their defenses. Her interventions were timely and appropriate. She developed rapport instantly, leading and pacing them toward the changes they desired. She put them in trances without any conscious awareness, and in a short time, transformations occurred. However, without boundaries or a mechanism to discharge toxic energy, it was just a matter of time until she broke down and the psychosis consumed her.

10

FIGHT OR FLIGHT

The earthquakes in Los Angeles, California, were the beginning of Pam's end. She would call me in the middle of the night with the terror of a little girl screaming for help. I was three thousand miles away, three hours later in time. I tried to calm her and give her advice on what to do, but the earthquakes seemed to have unhinged her illness. They became a metaphor of her internal state. They unnerved her, causing her to become fearful and phobic. To Pam the earthquakes were signs that the Devil was invading her home, searching her out, and making her his hostage. She believed he wanted her soul. She personalized her external experiences.

She needed to escape, to take refuge, but she couldn't leave all that she had built and worked so hard to achieve. The desire to flee began to haunt her night after night, and she could find no refuge or safe place in the city she loved. She was under the care of a psychiatrist and a psychologist, but no one seemed to be able to help her. She was decompensating, losing her grip, and on the way to having another breakdown.

Every evening brought another nightmare. She couldn't sleep and feared for her life. I told her she could return to Florida, although I was ambivalent about this. I was afraid she would one day regret it and resent me for telling her to do it. Her work, her friendships, and her life were in California. But it soon became apparent that there was no other choice except to return to Florida, where she'd grown up.

Pam came home hoping to be healed. At thirty-one years old, she had been away for nearly fifteen years. She thought she would fit back into the system. She thought she would be welcomed as if she were the prodigal daughter; however, our family dynamics had changed. We had all moved on. I had married again. Her sisters and brothers were living their own lives. Her expectations were not realized and she soon became depressed.

I gave her a space in my suite of offices. I referred clients to her so she was able to work. Then she began to think that I was cheating her out of money she had earned. She was temperamental and angry with me most of the time. She felt I didn't give her enough time, I had abandoned her, and I didn't care about her. Her laundry list was endless.

She asked me to go into therapy with her, so we attended a few sessions together. I realized that her anger and disappointment with me was something I could not repair. I also understood that the illness had taken its toll on her self-esteem and well-being.

She was diagnosed with bipolar I disorder after she returned to Florida. Her doctor placed her on mood stabilizers, as well as an antipsychotic agent and an antidepressant and regulated her medicine, but her symptoms persisted. I am not sure if she was noncompliant with her medication or if she was reactive to it.

I read books on mental disorders. I read about schizophrenia and affective disorders. I studied borderline personality disorder and the other personality disorders. Mostly I read about bipolar I. I asked questions. I talked to my colleagues. I learned that there were two types of bipolar: I and II. Pam was diagnosed with bipolar I, the worst kind. In most cases medication is effective and the prognosis is good. Other patients with this illness function as long as they take their medication. This apparently did not work for Pam.

I read Kay Redfield Jamison's *The Unquiet Mind*. I was amazed to read that this woman, head of the department of psychology at John Hopkins University, suffers from bipolar I disorder. She is functioning and managing life in spite of this retched illness. Lithium works for her. Why didn't it worked for Pam? It was the same illness, with similar symptoms. Why didn't Pam respond? There were questions and more questions, but no answers.

Pam's condition continued to deteriorate. Her past wreckage was catching up with her. The numerous traffic tickets she'd received and never paid were creating legal problems. She had to appear in court. Getting there was monumental. She took a dry run just to feel more comfortable. I received a frantic call from her after she'd taken a wrong turn off the expressway on her way to the courthouse and ended up at the airport. Her paranoia kicked in. She thought that agents of the underground were going to abduct her. She was terrorized and begged me to come get her. I gave her instructions how to return home. She demanded that I escort her to the courthouse the following day. The next day while I drove her to the court, she insisted that we pass the airport so I could witness what she had seen the day before. She had to prove it was not a hallucination as I had suggested. As I pulled up the perimeter road, she began to cry out.

"There they are! There they are!"

"What is there?" I asked.

"The airplanes that are not supposed to be there. There they are again," she cried, pointing to a plane in the hangar. "They're the ones that are going to take me away."

I tried to console her, explaining that it was Varig the Argentinean airline. I tried to reason with her, but she had difficulty understanding that it was normal to have foreign carriers in an international airport.

By the time we entered the courthouse, she was composed and attended to the matter without incident. Like a switch had been flipped; suddenly, she was lucid. Her thoughts were normal. She was able to respond appropriately to questions from the judge.

I never knew what to expect from her, and I struggled trying to help her. Her delusions had caused estrangement between us. There were times she believed I was part of the conspiracy in her psychotic belief system. In an effort to protect myself, I began to detach from her. This caused her more anxiety and anger. I could do no right.

It was then that she reached out to Kevin for love and support. Marriage seemed like her best hope for a rescue. After a rocky and brief courtship, they married. Three months later, she was again hospitalized with bizarre persecutory delusions.

She believed that she, as an agent between God and the Devil, was given a final test, a last opportunity "to redeem herself" and prove herself worthy in God's eyes. Pam believed she was to confront someone in her group therapy, but she did not do it. During this last hospitalization, she concluded that she'd failed that test. Her punishment would be that the Devil would take her soul. I tried many times to understand why she thought she'd failed.

Her explanation made no sense to me. She was riddled with guilt and shame from incidents in her past. Pam had acted out in a deviant manner, but when she was reflective and lucid she felt shameful about her behavior. When she was in undergraduate school, in a sorority, there was a girl who lived in the sorority house who had been suffering from a severe eating disorder. Pam had gone into the girl's room and discovered she had hidden popcorn under her bed. Out of compulsion, Pam urinated on the popcorn.

No matter what, nothing warranted such self-deprecation and punishment. She never told her doctors about this final test. It seems that this "final test" was something none of us could possibly understand or accept.

She was to be released four days after she was admitted. The night before her discharge, the staff heard her screaming in her room for Jesus to come and save her. The social worker on the unit who was working the night shift called me early in the morning to report this behavior and inquire if it had occurred before. She then informed me that my daughter would be released that morning. I was appalled. I couldn't believe a doctor would discharge a patient who was so profoundly out of touch with reality and in such a psychotic state. I made every effort to abort the discharge, but the administrator insisted that the doctor who had written the order for discharge did not believe Pam required further hospitalization. I demanded to speak with her psychiatrist, her fifth or sixth by now. I would not let her leave until I had heard from him. He confirmed what the administrator had told me, so I asked that another psychiatrist examine her. The second psychiatrist's assessment and recommendation was the same. Both had been on the panel of her HMO plan. I begged the administrator to keep her as a private patient, but she gave me a lot of administrative corporate babble that meant she could not keep Pam.

After much persuasion and my oath to hold them accountable and responsible for anything that might happen, the administrator reluctantly agreed to allow her to stay a few more days at my expense. I was relieved, but not for long. She demonstrated no change when she was finally discharged. She was still delusional and terrified. I felt so helpless. I was angry with the doctors, the hospital, the disease, the HMO, the whole goddamn system. I felt powerless, afraid, and unable to do anything to help my daughter.

I took her home with me for a brief time, but she became severely mistrustful of me. Her delusions continued. She said that she saw demons around me. I tried to reason with her, but to no avail. In her lucid moments she was able to understand my concerns and fears, but her paranoia would always intrude and interfere with any semblance of logic that remained. She said that she could not stay with me, that it was unbearable. So she moved in with her sisters one mile away. But they both worked and could not be there to make her feel safe. She left soon after to stay with Kevin, who had by now disassociated himself from her and the marriage.

A few months later when Pam and I returned from our trip to Israel, she declared that she wanted to leave Kevin. I urged her to try to work things out and be patient with him. I told her that her illness had put a strain on both him and the marriage. She was insistent. She complained that he was unable to understand her needs and to be loving and supportive. I understood both positions—hers and his. I met with Kevin several times alone and several times with our family in an effort to help him understand the illness. He was overwhelmed with fear and mistrust and unable to handle her disease and its manifestations. One could hardly blame him. He was eager to terminate the marriage.

Pam left Kevin and moved in with us. Angry and full of regret that she had married him, she blamed him for not being able to understand the nature of her illness. She was angry that he could not care for her. But he could not meet her needs and was not able to take care of her. Neither could anyone else.

On her first anniversary of her marriage to Kevin and three months before her death, Pam left me again. Her fears and hallucinations became intolerable. She had difficulty trusting me. I lived on the twelfth floor of a high-rise and I was frightened when I discovered her alone on the terrace. In a way, I was relieved when she told me she had to leave. She wanted to be with her sisters again. She felt safe with them.

She changed psychiatrists once more. This one would be her last. This time she chose an orthodox Jewish woman who was not on her HMO plan. Her father and I helped cover the fees. Her father had never denied her financial help. I did the best I could to help. I joined her in a few sessions, hoping against hope that perhaps this doctor would find answers. Medication and support were all she could provide. She suggested that Pam begin therapy with one of her colleagues, a clinical psychologist not on the plan either. Pam changed therapists often. She projected her delusions onto them. No one seemed able to control the disease. It had an agenda of its own.

Questions haunted me: When would my daughter recover? When could I sleep through the night? I called everyone I knew in the profession, including close friends who were psychiatrists and psychologists. They all responded alike, offering only one remedy: the medication, and she had them all. She was either sleeping for hours, day upon day, in a drugged state, or she was racing with thoughts of damnation and the Devil. We were spinning our wheels, draining our pockets and spirits. I researched possible in-patient facilities for long-term treatment. There weren't any available, certainly none with her HMO, and none that we could afford or that would even accept her. I tried the Menninger Institute in Kansas, but she didn't meet their criteria. I exhausted all possibilities. I couldn't believe there was no place she could go. Hopelessness became my unwanted companion.

My other daughters pleaded with me. "Mom, you have to do something!" I didn't know what to do or where to go. I kept running into the same response. Pam did not meet criteria for in-patient care. She seemed to be able to interview in ways that made her appear normal. She denied being suicidal and had enough knowledge of psychology to answer the questions in such a way as to not cause her therapists concern. I was told that Pam had a right to be crazy, but as long as she did not harm herself or others, hospitalization was not an option. She could be treated on an out-patient basis by her doctors.

I was frustrated, angry, and out of options. The bane of my existence had been the health care system. There were no doors open to her, no place for her to get help, nothing but dead ends. My two younger daughters and I were mentally and physically exhausted. They had been around-the-clock nursemaids for her and were being affected by her illness and unreasonable demands.

It was just four months before I took my sabbatical that I discovered Love Connection, the dating site where I met Jim. I rented the cabin in North Carolina for us in July. The distraction would be a welcome diversion from the painful ordeal with Pam.

As July drew near, Pam expressed a wish to go with us to the mountains. I was ambivalent about taking her. I feared her illness would take up all my time and attention, as it had in Israel. I originally agreed to take her along with us but then decided against it. She needed to be close to her doctor. Her father and Astrid would be her custodians for the time we were to be away.

On Monday, June 29, 1998, I flew to Wisconsin to meet Jim. I called Pam on Tuesday morning to see how she was feeling. Then I called her psychiatrist to see if she believed Pam would hurt herself. After being assured that the doctor would pay close attention for any signs during their next session, I left for North Carolina on Wednesday morning, and arrived at Beech Mountain on Thursday, close to midnight. Pam was already dead.

PART III

❧⌒⌒⌒⌒❧

11

THREE YEARS LATER

December 2001

I was somewhere in the Atlantic Ocean off the coast of
Central America, cruising aboard a luxury ocean liner
toward Costa Rica. Relaxing on the deck in a chaise
lounge, I closed the book I had been reading, then my eyes, and
finally my mind. I slipped into a light trance, envisioning in my
mind's eye the Twin Towers. I began to reflect on the events
of September 11. I asked myself the question that millions
of people must have asked: Where was God? That thought
reverberated over and over again in my mind. Everything else
disappeared. All I could hear was Where was God? Like a

mantra, it resounded over and over again. Where was God? Where was God? I lay there listening to the words that seemed to resonate with the rhythm of the waves. Where was God? Where was God? Moments passed that seemed like hours.

Then something within me shifted. The answer materialized in the form of a revelation. It was as if a voice in the distance was speaking to me. Abraham had been asked to sacrifice his only son, Isaac, to prove his love of God. God had sacrificed his only son, Jesus, to prove his love for all his children. He had once been so angry that he nearly destroyed all he had created, to make us more in his own image. He abandoned us to teach us not to abandon him. How many times have we seen his wrath? How many times did he try to communicate with us without results? What was he trying to teach us? Why was each lesson harder to learn than the previous one? What was the message in the Tower of Babel? What was it in Sodom and Gomorrah? Did he not hand us a set of instructions on how to live our lives? How many times had he failed, and how many times had we failed? When were we going to get it?

These esoteric thoughts kept pouring into my semiconscious mind. I opened my eyes only to realize that I was still on the deck and only a few minutes had passed. Somewhat perplexed by this process, I wondered why these thoughts came into my consciousness. The message was familiar. I had heard it before. My girlfriend Lorraine had once shared her thoughts with me. A Catholic, she'd made many trips to Mejagora to a sighting of the Virgin Mary. She often spoke about the messages Mary had given to some local children at the time of her appearance. All pertained to the need of getting closer to God. I had heard some recent discussions on National Public Radio in an open forum with rabbis, priests, and Muslim clerics. They addressed the "Where was God?" question. Then I remembered Pam's message before she had died. She had felt split off from God, that they had abandoned each another. This became her fear. Would he hear her? Would he save her from forces she could not elude? I could hear her pleas. She had warned me of an evil yet to come that would change the world forever. I wondered if it was her voice that I heard in the distance.

Those of us in the world of "sanity," especially the psychiatric community, believe that those who are mentally disturbed have hallucinations, which are a symptom of the illness. Taking the correct dosage of the appropriate medication often diminishes or perhaps suppresses these hallucinations or delusions; however, I sometimes wonder if patients who suffer from mental disorders like schizophrenia and bipolar disorder have some sixth sense that those of us who are considered normal never experience. I certainly have no empirical evidence of this seemingly preposterous notion. I can only wonder. When I consider all the nonempirical data and listen to the sounds of my soul and the refrains of my heart, I can't help but wonder and even consider the possibility that all this may exist.

I have conversations with my angel every day. I recall these communications, sometimes in retrospect after significant events occur. I find it puzzling that I have been able to actualize almost all of my hopes, wishes, and dreams since my daughter left this earth. I often wonder if perhaps she is working some miracles from above. My life has moved forward in a fashion that most people can only dream about. We all want health, happiness, security, and love. We all seek answers to our questions, solutions to our problems, and wisdom not to repeat the patterns and choices that have caused pain and conflict.

At the time of Pam's death, I was alone. Jim had been there for the moment and provided a supportive role, but it came with a high price. The timing was bad. Grief requires moments of solitude and time to feel. Both need special attention. Love and grief don't mix. It's nearly impossible to possess energy for both. Grief demanded most of my time and effort, and whatever was left I needed for survival and healing.

I always wanted a healthy relationship. My history is not good. I experienced many painful breakups, many disappointments. I believed that I would not be alone forever, that I would eventually find someone loving and caring who could be my life partner. I wanted a relationship with someone who could share my values and interests. Deep down I didn't expect it to happen, and I was okay with that. Yet I yearned for a partner to share my remaining years.

Five months after Pam's death, I found the man who I thought was my soul mate. We were together three and a half years. Those years together helped heal my sorrow and grief.

My son and daughter-in-law had been trying to conceive a child for about a year. During the week of Pam's shiva, my granddaughter was conceived. Despite my belief that Todd's career choice was only to satisfy his father and grandfather's wishes, he maintains a successful and rewarding practice.

Aaron's early childhood hip slippage that caused a permanent disability and a severe limp, coupled with his adolescent obesity, affected his sense of self-worth and confidence. Alone for most of his life, he often wondered if there was a soul mate for him. He confided in me soon after Pam's death that he had "let it go." In his words, "If it happens, Mom, then it will happen. If not, I will accept my destiny." Only days later he met the woman who would become his wife. They had a son in May 2002, and a daughter in December 2005.

My daughter Erika, eager to find love and marriage, became engaged nine months after Pam died. She often recalled the words Pam would say to her, "Your time will come, Erika. Be patient and it will come." It seemed as if Pam's words came true. She and her husband have a three-month old daughter, Pamella Shae, whom they call Ella. Two more children, a boy and a girl followed.

My daughter Monica has become the person she was intended to be. She has carved out a fulfilling and rewarding lifestyle. It seems as if she integrated Pam into her own soul and spirit. The healthy part of Pam seems to live on in Monica. She moves with grace and confidence. She believes that her sister is always with her. It is amazing to me that all this could have happened in so short a time.

In Pam's last note she wrote the night before she died, she spoke of when she could she give back. Perhaps she has, even more in death than in life. All of us were absorbed in Pam's care and safety to the extent that our own lives were more or less placed on hold during the last three years of her life. Yet I feel her presence. I hear her thoughts. I see her smile. Mostly in my dreams I do all of this. But dream stuff is where she can reside in comfort.

I can breathe now. My life has taken on new meaning. This does not mean her memory has faded. Instead, the child I once knew has returned. I can celebrate her life. I see her at play now. I see her in her tutu and tights and trying to squeeze into a pair of jeans that no longer fit. I hear her giggling with her siblings and shouting cheers in cheerleading practice. I feel her come into my bed at night after a bad dream. I feel her soft touch on my hair, her gentle kiss, her loving arms around my neck, and her tight hug just before she boards the train to camp. I smell her sweet breath in the night. I hear her sobbing after her first boyfriend broke her heart. I hear her infectious laughter and watch her looking in the mirror, trying endlessly to make her cheeks hallow by sucking them in and pursing her lips. I remember her healing her wounded clients with fervor and grace. I recall our walks, her smiles, her warmth, and her silliness with a fondness. I know she will never leave me. I am healing. Time is my friend. My life has new meaning. Her death has new meaning. <u>She has left us all a legacy of love,</u> not of suicide.

My search for healing took me to a place where I could create a center in her name. The Pamela Ann Glassman Educational

Center provides information and resources for anyone who needs help in Broward County. I have produced a television series called *Solutions,* consisting of twenty-four one-half hour shows on mental health, which I dedicated to my daughter. Each program deals with a different topic on mental health, including depression, bipolar disorder, divorce, anxiety, relationship issues, and more. By giving meaning to her memory, my life also took on new meaning. I discovered myself once more. I had something to offer the community, and Pam's death created new life in me as a community activist and advocate for mental health.

I have worked long and hard on healing and found professional and personal support important for grieving. Professional support offered me a safe place to express my feelings. It allowed them to be honored and acknowledged. It provided an experience to mourn and feel. It offered an opportunity to learn that grieving is normal and healthy. It allowed for the process to move along and facilitated my healing.

Time changes things, even the grieving. And as time passes, so does the pain. Time has not altered the memories. Time has not eroded my images. I remember the best and no longer think of the worst.

12

SIX YEARS LATER

July 2, 2004

I t was easy to recognize July. The humidity hung heavy with little wind to diffuse its effect. The drive to the cemetery seemed longer than had the last trip in October. This time Monica sat next to me in the passenger seat. It was the first time she'd attended our small family gathering over the graveside since the funeral. She had visited her sister's grave only on Pam's birthday, never on the day she passed.

It was difficult for Monica. A shadow fell on her birthday every year since Pam had died—only two days after Monica's birthday. Her birthdays were never the same again. This one had been no better, except thirty of her friends and family members had joined her the night before to celebrate. No matter how cheerful the night, the memory of Pam's passing infiltrated.

"Yizkor elohim nishmas beetee hayekarah Pinina shehalacha l'oama, baavoor."

Paul chanted the same Hebrew words that he'd chanted the seven nights of shiva. How many times had we chanted the Kaddish, the Hebrew prayer for the dead, I wondered. How many more times would we recite them, standing, heads bowed, with the same heaviness in our hearts that never seemed to go away and probably never would? We'd lived with it so long now that it was an integral part of our being. We treated it as a friendly reminder that we once had a daughter and a sister. In a way, none of us ever wanted that heaviness to go away. The reminder was somehow comforting.

I looked at their faces. Why did they have to suffer this loss in their youth? How had this impacted their lives for better or for worse? What lessons did they learn about life? What difference had Pam's death made in their lives? I didn't expect an answer to these familiar questions. I wondered if they ever reflected on these questions or if they were only my own projections. We hardly spoke of her death anymore. When we spoke of Pam, we shared the past with good memories. I assumed this was good. Perhaps we had finally come to accept her death. "Remember the time . . . ?" or "Remember when Pam . . . ?" This seemed to bring us closer together. Sharing stories, laughter, and even heartbreak seemed to cement our familiar ties even closer.

I planted an oak tree as a memorial to her in Valle Crucis Park, North Carolina, a place she would have loved. It was planted next to the Wautauga River, so when we visit, we hear the sound of the river as we rededicate our remembrance and love. We prefer to think of her there, and not in her grave. The plaque reads:

IN LOVING MEMORY

OF

PAMELA ANN GLASSMAN

AN ANGEL TO REMEMBER

I glanced at Paul. He donned the traditional yarmulke worn on occasions such as this. His hair was more salt than pepper now. He brought flowers to the site. He gently placed them all around the bronze headstone identifying our daughter's grave. I glanced down. I read it again. The words were true:

PAMELA (PININA) ANN GLASSMAN

SHE TOUCHED MANY PEOPLE IN

WAYS FEW OTHERS HAD.

Paul had the words inscribed when he ordered the footstone. I first saw it when we held the unveiling on that auspicious day about a year after she'd passed when we consecrated her grave with the stone, as is the custom in our religion. Until then, her grave had remained unmarked. I began to realize the value of some of our Jewish traditions and how they helped us deal with the loss of a loved one. Every custom seemed rich in value. The rituals and customs gave us time to heal and time to join our sorrow together to appreciate our blessings and realize the finiteness of life. I think it gave us a conscious awareness that usually comes with matura-tion and aging. Life seemed to matter more. We all developed an appreciation for living life in the moment.

I studied Paul as he recited the prayer. He wore his years well. He had suffered two angioplasties, the most recent included the insertion of a stent to keep the artery open and hopefully prevent another blockage.

Aging has its way of rearing its ugly head to all of us, often when we least expect it. The aches and pains that I had always heard others complain about were now permeating my daily existence. I fought them with a vengeance. But in spite of working out three or four times a week, they never let me forget them. Perhaps without the effort, it might be worse.

I examined my life over these last six years after Pam's passing. I had the usual ups and downs shared by so many others my age. Still single, living alone was not my idea of happiness; but having a mate who was not right for me was not an acceptable resolution. After the termination of my four-year relationship with David, things had not gone so well for me. It had been one of the most traumatic events in my life. I was sixty-two when David formally discharged me from the relationship. He caught me by great surprise when he announced that he wanted to be free. No discussion. He had made up his mind and I had to leave the home I had created for us. I had nowhere to go, because I had foolishly given up my home to share my life with him. My naiveté and trusting nature never would have believed that this could happen. My thoughts shifted to the day he had told me.

The weekend had been glorious. We'd shared Friday evening and Saturday with good friends. My life seemed safe and predictable.

I'd met David only five months after Pam passed away. I was just coming out of shock. David seemed magical. He swept me off my feet. It broke my grief state and I was eager to feel love in my heart once again. I knew that David was not interested in marriage. He had made that quite clear from the get-go. Living together was a reasonable alternative, so I accepted his choice with disappointment but with full commitment.

Sunday followed uneventfully. Monica needed a special dress for her friend's wedding. I invited her to choose from one of mine, because I had so many. David asked her to stay for dinner. I prepared pasta and salad, which I served on the terrace. She modeled the dresses for us. David shared his comments and chose the one he liked best. We laughed, sang songs, and lay on the large lounge chair—he in the center with his arms around us both. Life seemed so settled. I was happy and he appeared to be happy also.

He had been suffering from chest pains for a few weeks, accompanied with a body rash. He minimized the chest pains, hoping they would disappear. He'd had an angioplasty some years before

I met him, so he felt confident that the symptoms would dissipate uneventfully. I encouraged him to see a cardiologist, but he refused, each time giving derogatory remarks regarding the lack of integrity in the medical profession. I suggested he see a dermatologist for the rash. After a few weeks without any relief, he made an appointment. He was convinced that the chest pains were unremarkable. The dermatologist diagnosed it as poison ivy. I was surprised, wondering where he could have contacted it.

David asked Monica to stay the night. She happily agreed. We said our good-byes to her early the next morning as she was leaving.

"David, I hope you and Mommy will grow old together," she said.

"We will, Monica. We will," he said reassuringly.

Monica kissed us good-bye and then drove off. We both showered together, which was our custom. We dressed and I made some tea. We kissed and said our good-byes. The day was no different from any other Monday. He picked up his briefcase and shouted his good-byes once more, announcing he would see me later.

These last few years had not been easy for the world. It was only six months after 9/11. Israel was struggling with the Palestine uprisings. Each day brought more suicide bombings and loss of lives. Most of David's family lived in Israel. His heritage and history made it impossible for him to ignore these events, even though he had lived in this country more than twenty-five years. He was glued to the giant television screen every evening. He turned it on the moment he entered the house. He never spoke much. He just watched with interest, sharing comments only when I asked a question. Most of his responses were short and negative.

"It doesn't matter. In ten or twenty years, there will be no Israel." His brevity seemed cold. His affect was always flat and unemotional. Yet, that set went on every evening without fail.

"Perhaps you shouldn't watch it so often," I said. "Maybe it causes you too much stress." Usually, he never replied.

David owned and operated several restaurants in several counties about fifty minutes north of the house. He had been in the restaurant business for many years, always successful. He had a knack for negotiating and creating a good product. I admired his savvy and business acumen. I was proud that like many Israelis he came to this country with nothing and created a dynasty, without having anything ever handed to him. He earned it all by himself. He developed a tough persona. His armor and arrogance had long been in place from learning to survive in a land of daily threats. Although his attitude helped him survive in Israel, Americans perceived these attributes differently. His strong personality came across as arrogant and self-righteous. He took liberties that were often politically incorrect, sounding chauvinistic, patriarchal, and often even racist. He had a quick temper and no tolerance for what he determined to be stupidity. He could be cruel to others and especially to me. I tried to sweep his behavior under the carpet in order to live peacefully and avoid conflicts. This was a mistake. I knew better than to subjugate my feelings to a man. For some reason, I let him get away with abusive behavior, rationalizing that it was his way, the only way he knew. Now I realized I was just responding out of fear that he would leave me if I ever challenged him. I sometimes wonder if codependency ever leaves us. After all these years of being a therapist, expounding on the knowledge of this illness to myself, my clients and others, there still seems to be a residue that casts its shadows even this late in life.

I came home that Monday evening and found him in bed, his hands clutching his chest. His face was screwed up, and visibly uncomfortable.

"Perhaps you should see the cardiologist," I said.

"No, I am not seeing any cardiologist!"

"David, this could be very dangerous. After all, you are past sixty and have already had an angioplasty. You could be looking for trouble." I was worried. I finally convinced him to speak with a neighbor cardiologist, who convinced him to go to his office first thing in the morning. Reluctantly, he agreed.

When I'd moved in with David, I moved my office to be closer to his home—my third move in two years. I had worked in the same office on Hallandale Beach Boulevard since 1978, with a few exceptions. I came back to the Hallandale office after being in three different offices during the time I was involved with John Bradshaw. We had needed more space as the needs of the office expanded. It was there on Hallandale, where we established Joan Childs and Associates, an affiliate of the John Bradshaw Center. I met David five months after Pam's death. He encouraged me to move the office closer to home in Fort Lauderdale. My first move was too far west. I stayed there for one year. My second move was closer on Las Olas Boulevard in downtown Fort Lauderdale, but he felt that was too far away as well. The third and final move was to another location north of Las Olas on Sunrise. I still maintain a second office there today, along with my original location. David encouraged me to make these moves, feeling the drive between work and home would be easier.

"Would you like me to cancel my appointments for tomorrow so I can be with you? I can do that very easily," I said.

"No, I don't need you to go with me. I know the routine. They will run some blood tests, perform an EKG, and then send me home, only to return the following day for a stress test. I have been through this before. I know what to expect. I promise you, they will find nothing." He seemed so self-assured.

I went to work anxiously that Tuesday. He left for the doctor's office as promised. I worried about him all day and tried not to call him, knowing he would be busy with tests. On the way home I ruminated about his symptoms, wondering if they were stress related, as I believed they were. Having been a psychotherapist for many years, I clearly understood that the body responds to stress in a physical manner when issues are not resolved. We often referred to it as tissue issues: If the mind doesn't have enough sense to tell you to slow down, the body will.

David had many unresolved issues. He never believed in therapy, choosing instead to dissociate or repress whatever was disturbing to him by using rationalization and projection as a defense. "Feeling confident" and "moving forward" was always his answer. We were so different. One of his favorite comments that he repeated to me often was that psychology was bullshit. I would think, "Great, he thinks my life's work is bullshit!"

I arrived home and went into the bedroom, where I saw him lying as he had the night before. His hands were once again holding his chest. He looked tired. I went to his side, smiling, hoping that things had gone well.

"How are you, sweetheart?"

"I'm fine. I told you I would be fine," he said, tension cutting each word. "They are going to do more tests in the next few days. I don't have any results yet."

He seemed annoyed and agitated. I assumed it was the result of spending the day in the hospital and having gone through the seemingly endless tests.

"Look, let me speak to you for a moment as a therapist, not your girlfriend. I know that you think what I do for a living is bullshit, but just hear me out."

Surprisingly, he listened.

I shared my belief that perhaps his symptoms were a result of the many problems at one of his restaurants that he had been complaining about for weeks. I shared my thoughts about the problems that were persistent with one of his estranged daughters. I commented on the disturbing news about Israel and Palestine, as well as the recent chasm with his sister that had resulted in a complete breakdown in communication. All of these issues, coupled with the day-to-day machinations of running a restaurant were, perhaps, overloading his plate and causing anxiety that he may not have been in touch with.

He stared at me. "Well, what do you propose I do about all these things?"

"For one thing, you certainly don't need all this aggravation at work each day. Why don't you think about selling the restaurant? You don't need the income, and you are close to sixty-two. Perhaps some time off will do you good.

"As far as your daughter, maybe you should talk to me about her. Get it off your chest. She is and always will be your daughter. If you are suffering because of her behavior, at least talk about it. Sharing with a supportive and caring mate might help. And don't turn on the television set on every night. Give yourself some relief. You don't realize it, but hearing these atrocities night after night affects you. It may be contributing to your mood or causing you to be depressed without your even realizing it.

"And why don't you mend the fences with your sister? Try to make peace with her. I know you see things differently. You always have. But she is your sister, and it hurts you not to be speaking to each other. It's been over six months since your brother died. You need to settle your differences. Silence is not a good resolution."

It all made sense to me. I hoped I hadn't sounded as if I was lecturing. The words seem to tumble out of my mouth as if I had said the words a hundred times before. I was convinced I had said the right thing.

David glared at me. I could tell he was forming a retort. He

always had the same expression on his face when he thought I
made sense but he wanted to challenge me. He took a few deep
breaths. He spoke slowly. He changed the tenor of his voice. "I
don't give a shit about my daughter. She has always been a problem. She will always be a problem. I have to learn to live with it.
She is my daughter, but that does not mean I have to love her. The
restaurant, well, this is all part of the territory of being an owner.
I live with problems. That's not even an issue. Israel . . . is another
matter. There will soon not be an Israel. I can't concern myself with
a country that I have no control over. And my sister . . . the hell
with her! I didn't go to her son's wedding because I didn't like the
way she treated me after my brother died. She is competitive and
always needs to feel better than me. I am sick of it. I don't want to
see or hear from her again. She is not my sister!"

I was shocked, but I said nothing.

"And if you really want to know what is bothering me, I will tell
you. It's us! I am not happy and have not been happy for a year."

I thought I was going to faint. My chest swelled with what felt
like hot air. My eyes welled with tears. I began to quiver. I couldn't
believe what I was hearing. Suddenly my worst fear emerged. I
knew what was coming. I felt like a trapped rabbit. That was how
he operated. He waited for the right time to attack. When I was
most open and vulnerable, he made his move.

After a few responses, questions, and feeble attempts of trying
to understand, David said he wanted to end our relationship. He
asked me to move out as quickly as possible. Stunned, I was unable

to speak to ask him why. I just went upstairs to a guest bedroom, lay down, wept, and stayed awake that whole evening. The next morning was no better. I prayed that it was all just a nightmare. I was hoping we could work it out. But when I entered the kitchen to make the morning tea, his mood was surly and distant. It was his way of closing down. He was in his cave and there was no turning back. In less than twenty minutes, he shut me out of his heart, his life, and now his home. I knew that once that door closed between us, I would be no different from his daughter or his sister. I was no longer a part of his life. I never learned why and never heard from him again.

The sound of the chanting brought me back to the moment once more. How fast the years had gone. How many years would be left, and how would I live out these years, I wondered. My mind raced with existential thoughts as I heard each of us chant the prayers. When would my remaining children be standing over my grave and reciting the same prayers? I sounded like my parents. I shuddered at these maudlin thoughts.

So many changes in these last six years, I thought. The children aged along with me. Suddenly, I was aware how quickly six years had passed and noted that the next six would be even faster. I took stock of where I was that day. I was still practicing psychotherapy, creating and developing The Pamela Ann Glassman Educational Center along with the Dade County Mental Health Association, and later the Broward Mental Health Association, producing a television show to provide information and resources to the community on mental health, and just living my life.

I still don't have the answers, but I have become comfortable without them. I forgave myself for all the "what ifs." I forgave Pam and accepted her death as the only choice she had at that time. Strange as that may sound, it was her answer. That's all that really matters.

So what have I learned? What have these six years taught me? Have I really changed? Have I applied any of these lessons to my life in beneficial ways? Have my relationships with my children changed as a result of losing a daughter? Have I come to terms with living life on life's terms instead of always trying to plan ahead, control the variables, and play it safe? I think just asking these questions, philosophical as they are, is the first step in examining who and where I am, where I have been, and where I want to be.

I don't think I have really changed. I know that life is finite, so I have learned to treasure the moment. I have learned to count my blessings, including accepting that David discharged me from his life as perhaps one of the best things that ever happened. I have learned to be grateful for what I have as opposed to lamenting about what I don't have. I don't worry so much anymore. I still think about the future but swiftly return to the present. I don't care as much about what other people think. I care more about what I think rather than what others think, as I have come to realize that most people don't really think about me anyway.

I still make my bed every day. I pay my bills on time. I still love to shop at Bloomingdale's, but if I can't afford the blouse, I walk away and say, "Bloomie's will be here longer than I will. There will always be another blouse." I quote the same insipid platitudes my father quoted that used to irritate me. Now I find them meaningful and useful. I find myself saving more money than I used to spend, checking prices at the grocery store and buying generics more often. I wonder if that is a sign of old age. I listen more and talk less. I play more and work less. And if it were up to me, I would make love at least once a day. I smile at children, laugh and play with my grandchildren, and watch *The Golden Girls* before I retire each night (it brings me to a happy state). I sing in the shower, wear lots of sunscreen, and never hang up the phone without saying "I love you" when I speak to my kids.

Now when I look at Pam's photos, I remember her spirit. I think about the best of times we shared. I dream about her at least once a month. I say my prayers every night, get up at least twice during the night to go to the bathroom, and greet every day with a sense of wonder. I don't have too many expectations; therefore, I don't have too many disappointments. I see each day as a new adventure, and each moment as the best part of the day. No, I'm not a Pollyanna, just a woman who appreciates life and wants to live it until I die. This is what I have learned: to live each day as if it were my last, because one day it will be. It's easier this way. It gives me freedom, the freedom to have more energy to be. I guess it could be worse.

It has been nearly seven years now. I am approaching my sixty-sixth birthday. I've been a senior citizen for nearly one year. In the years that have passed since Pam's death, I have developed diabetes, become a grandmother three times—with another on the way—collected social security, maintained my private practice—albeit only three days a week—enjoyed a single life, and have never known a day without my angel in my thoughts.

13

FIFTEEN YEARS LATER

I t took seven years to write this book and nearly nine years have passed since I completed it. It wasn't until recently that Health Communications, Inc. accepted it for publishing, eight years after I had self-published. In these last nine years since I closed the manuscript, the grieving process took several turns. As grief and healing are different for each person, I can only reflect on my own experience, now fifteen years after Pam's death.

The question that is often asked is, "Does the pain ever go away?"

My stock answer has been, "Yes, and other things take its place." Thankfully, time does heal, although in the first stage of grief this statement will not console the griever. Memories, both bad and good emerge where only pain existed. She comes in my dreams. She appears as a butterfly when I am walking my dog, visiting her grave site, sitting by the tree I planted in North Carolina, or just suddenly, out of nowhere. I visit her when I am in synagogue praying, in places we went together, and when speaking to her friends and colleagues who still talk about her. The pain diminishes, but the memories remain.

I am often reminded of the quote I referred to earlier in the book that John Bradshaw so often shared with his audiences and readers: "There are places in the heart that do not yet exist. Pain must be in order that they be."

It makes sense to me now, after the loss. Before it just sounded like poetry, without personal reference. There is not a day that goes by that I don't think of Pam. I miss her every day!

Omar Khayyan writes,

The Moving Finger writes; and, having writ,
Moves on: nor all thy Piety nor Wit
Shall lure it back to cancel half a Line,
Nor all thy Tears wash out a Word of it. "The moving finger writes,
and having writ, moves on . . ."

This sums it up. I came to realize that I did everything possible with the resources I had at the time. I came to realize that I couldn't turn back the hands of time. I came to accept that this was

Pam's destiny and neither "all the king's horses and all the king's men could put her back together again." My daughter is gone and nothing will bring her back. It took years to get my brain wrapped around that truth. It took years to come to terms with the reality of her death. There was a moment when I had to choose between being a victim or being a survivor. I chose to survive!

I learned to forgive; forgive myself for what I thought I could have done and didn't; forgive the professionals and health system for failing her by allowing her to fall through the cracks. I forgave Pam for taking her life and leaving us without warning, without a good-bye or an explanation. I came to understand her disease and accept it as a physiological illness not unlike brain cancer. Most of all, I forgave God for taking her from us. I accepted his will and believe that she is resting in peace and in a better place.

Her photographs hang and stand in my home along with all my other children and grandchildren. There are no shrines that signify her loss. The only memorial is the oak tree in Valle Crucis, North Carolina, that is a place for us to go to commemorate and celebrate her life and the love she gave to all of us. Her death prompted the writing of this book as a way of dealing with the interminable pain of grief, but now in hope that it will give insight and understanding to those who are experiencing what I experienced and meaning to her life. It forged the opening of a center where professionals can present their theories and programs to the public to help educate and inform people about mental illness and provide resources for them.

Bipolar I disorder carries no preferences. It attacks the rich, the poor, all races, all religions, and all creeds. It knows no boundaries regarding intelligence, gender, sexual preference, or nationality. In other words, you and your families are all open targets for this insidious disease that can strike at any time to anyone. Of all the organs in our bodies, the one we know the least about is the brain. That is why some medications will work effectively with some of the people some of the time, some of the people all of the time, but not all of the people all of the time. We know that many hosts of this illness will take their lives and it will usually be characterized by violence. This is not uncommon. We know that many substance addictions are ways of managing feelings and when abstinence occurs, we can usually find another diagnosis beneath the addiction, and many times it is bipolar I disorder. We now know that 4 percent of American adults suffer from bipolar disorder I and II and it is often a precursor to suicide.

The latest statistics that were published in the *New York Times* and written by Tara Parker Pope reveal that "more people now die of suicide than in car accidents, according to the Centers for Disease Control and Prevention, which published the findings in its Morbidity and Mortality Weekly Report on May 2, 2003. In 2010 there were 33,687 deaths from motor vehicle crashes and 38,364 suicides.

"Suicide has typically been viewed as a problem of teenagers and the elderly, and the surge in suicide rates among middle-aged

Americans is surprising. From 1999 to 2010, the suicide rate among Americans ages 35 to 64 rose by nearly 30 percent, to 17.6 deaths per 100,000 people, up from 13.7. Although suicide rates are growing among both middle-aged men and women, far more men take their own lives. The suicide rate for middle-aged men was 27.3 deaths per 100,000, while for women it was 8.1 deaths per 100,000.

"The most pronounced increases were seen among men in their 50s, a group in which suicide rates jumped by nearly 50 percent, to about 30 per 100,000. For women, the largest increase was seen in those ages 60 to 64, among whom rates increased by nearly 60 percent, to 7.0 per 100,000."

Still, we don't have the answer as to why or what. We believe that there is a genetic predisposition to this illness. We believe that there is hope for managing it. Most of the problem lies in our substandard health system. We have yet to find a way to get an early diagnosis due to the comorbidity, a way to pay for mental health care, a way to provide sufficient insurance benefits for psychiatric illnesses and, worse yet, to find a safe place where patients can have long-term care without horrific costs. That will be the solution. When that occurs, it will hopefully stop the violence that filters through our culture and help establish and maintain a safer environment for all of us.

We must educate the public so they can find help and support for this condition. With the onslaught of children being diagnosed on the spectrum of autism, we need to understand if this might be a precursor to this diagnosis. We still know so little. I sometimes wonder if we are going through a mutation of a new species of humans. When we look back over history, we find that man had to adapt to the environment. We evolved over time as "the survival of the fittest." I wonder if the children being born into the twenty-first century are "the star children" or "the Indigo children," a new evolved species of children who are preparing and adapting to the change of time in the world of technology. Technology is moving so fast that humans may have to find a way to keep up with it, and the spectrum may be the sign of the time. None of the above has been substantiated and documented by empirical data. They are just my gut feelings, albeit, science is identifying these changes as this book is being published. I have three grandchildren who have been diagnosed on the spectrum. Each one of them exhibits what has been termed "Indigo Children." They may be the future generation of "the brave new world" in their own inimitable fashion.

As for myself, I am still maintaining a private practice. I still live alone and have a significant other. I spend my spare time traveling or chilling in North Carolina where I find the time to continue to write. I give lectures, presentations, and seminars on mental illness and share my story with the public whenever I have an opportunity, a sort of spokesperson for bipolar I disorder. I believe that this book, although written by me, was channeled by Pam.

One last thought: "We find a place for what we lose. Although we know that after such a loss the acute stage of mourning will subside, we also know that a part of us shall remain inconsolable and never find a substitute. No matter what may fill the gap, even if it is completely filled, it will nevertheless remain something changed forever."

—*Sigmund Freud*

14

AN ANGEL TO REMEMBER

Pam's life was truncated. She left us before she had a chance to find herself, to heal herself, and to be productive in a world she both loved and feared. Most of this book was about her illness. I wish also to memorialize the joy and love she brought to so many others. Her talent, her creativity, and her attachment to her family and friends were just a small part of who she was.

I can see Pam in Gustav Klimt's painting *Danae*. I see her sensuous eyes closed, her naked body curled in sleep, revealing her magnificent thighs and her long golden brown hair cascading loosely over her shoulders. She is Danae.

I can hear her in the poetry of Leonard Cohen's "Suzanne" as "she takes you down by the river, to see the boats go by, and feeds you tea and oranges that come all the way from China." She is Suzanne.

I hear her in the music of The Beatles' "Something in the Way She Moves." They could have written it of her. I hear her in John Lennon's "Imagine." I smell her in a summer rose or in the jasmine that sometimes suffuses the evening summer air. I see her in a butterfly dancing with the wind when I am sitting on my terrace or visiting her graveside. I hear her in the laughter of children, in their songs, and in their monologues, especially when I am with my granddaughter. I see her in the rainbows, in the clouds, and in the seagulls that gently sweep the shores I walk upon. I feel her in the balmy breezes that cool me on my walks. I watch a movie and appreciate her response as if she were beside me in the theater. She would have loved *Moulin Rouge,* hated *A Beautiful Mind,* and adored *Amalie.* She would have had much to say about *Silver Linings Playbook* as not being realistic. Her comment might have been, "You can't dance your way through bipolar I disorder!" She would have cried for the suffering and grief our country sustained on 9/11. She would have wept for the nation, mourned for the families and friends, and prayed for the children who lost their parents. She would have been devastated over the horrors of Sandy Hook and the Boston Marathon and would have never been able to cope with the slaughter of innocent lives both here on our own soil and abroad. She would never have been able to get over the tragedies that have befallen our country. Her gentle soul could never have withstood it. Perhaps that is why God brought her home: to spare her of the evil she seemed to fear and know so well. She will always be remembered, as will all of those who are gone.

Pam is my angel. Angels live forever. She is eternal and will be remembered by her friends, her lovers, her siblings, her daddy, her patients, and her foes. Even at her worst, she radiated a goodness that outshined all her ills. She gave the world a gift of love that will not be forgotten.

To her family, she was a teacher. She provided guidance, support, and timeless energy. She was never jealous of anyone. She was proud of all her siblings. She was happy for their joys and successes. They will remember how she lied to protect them. They will remember when she read to them and sang to them. They will remember the safety she provided them. They will always remember their sister.

To her lovers, she was their goddess. She made them feel like heroes and lions. She lifted them up to heights far above their boundaries. She dared to give them all of herself. For some she was, perhaps, too much. For a few, she was all they had hoped to find. She challenged their minds, their bodies, and their sexuality. Together they reached awareness. They will never forget her.

To her friends she gave her time, her knowledge, and her patience. They tell me she comes to them in their dreams. They can still see her clearly. They remember her generosity, her effort, and her deeds. They will always remember her friendship.

To her patients she gave new life and hope. She taught them how to live a new way. She cleaned and tended their wounded hearts and spirits. She renewed their faith and trust in others. She made them strong when they thought they were weak. She gave them hope when they had none. They will always remember their therapist.

Her daddy was her hero. He adored her. He remembers the night she was born, her first cry, and her first smile. He remembers when she ran to the door to announce his return home. He remembers the times she crawled up onto his lap and wrapped her arms around his neck, kissing him over and over again, telling him she would marry him when she grew up. He remembers how she gazed into his eyes with love and gratitude as she became a Bat Mitzvah. He remembers how she looked as she twirled around in her evening dress before she left with her date for the senior prom. He remembers his tears when her radiance overcame him. He remembers how she put her arm around his waist and danced with him to the sounds of the Hasapiko at the Greek Tavernas. He remembers her graduations with paternal pride and hope in his heart. He remembers the day he walked her down the aisle to the refrains of "Is this the little girl I carried?" He will always remember his firstborn, his little girl.

Pam lives in the hearts and minds of all who loved her. She continues to be a part of our daily lives. Her being influenced us and showered upon us the love and light that will be a part of us always. She taught us to forgive and love ourselves. We will always be grateful to her. We will always remember our angel.

15

THE CABIN IN
THE GLEN

I once owned an old cabin in a glen, off Highway 194
between Banner Elk and Valle Crucis, North Carolina.
The cabin was nestled in a pasture that was adorned with
multiple trees indigenous to the Blue Ridge Mountains. There
were North Carolina pine, chestnut, evergreen, oak, maple, white
birch, spruce, and more. To borrow a phrase from Isaac Beshevis
Singer, "The trees were as tall and straight as pillars and the
sky leaned on their green tops. Brooches, rings, gold coins were
embossed on the bark of their trunks. The earth, carpeted with
moss and other vegetation, gave off an intoxicating odor." It's
hard to imagine that two places on earth, so far from each other,
could be so alike.

Isaac Beshevis Singer, *The Slave* (New York: Farrar, Straus and Giroux, 1988).

A creek filled with hundreds of rocks flowed through two col-
umns of trees that made the brook sing as it traveled along into a
culvert emptying into a pond on the other side of the road. That
creek seemed to sing all the time, season after season, never changing its song; neither in winter, summer, spring, nor fall.

To reach the cabin, you had to hang a left off the two-lane
crooked highway, onto a dirt road, and drive about an eighth of a
mile past two ponds until you reached a pasture where the cabin
still stood since the mid-nineteenth century. I made the tragic
choice to give it up in a divorce settlement in 1997, a decision I
have always regretted.

That cabin has never left my heart. It was the only piece of
property that I ever had an attachment for and have always had
dreams of owning once more. Everyone who has ever lived in
Avery or Watauga counties knew about that cabin. It looked
like a piece of sculpture in space. Thick old logs, hand-hewn,
duck-tailed, and devoid of nails revealed the cabin's authenticity. A shanty, sloped roof line covered with weathered shingles
shared space with the porch that bore old vertical logs serving
as support beams. I had the best years of my life in that cabin
in the glen, set in an apple orchard long before it became a
small development and lost some of its charm soon after I left.
There are some things in our hearts and minds that, no matter how
many years go by, never leave you. I would sit on the porch of that
cabin in a very old swing I had purchased from a very old couple
who had had that swing since they were first married, given to

them by the woman's parents who had had it since they had been married. That swing stood untouched, frozen in time, weathered and worn since its beginning. I would sit there and rock in that swing for what might have been hours, facing infinity, mesmerized, falling into a trance watching the golden finch flock around the feeder near the brook that surrounded the pasture where my cabin lived in history for perhaps more than a century and a half. I could feel its age on my pulse, as if I had drifted back into that time.

Peacocks would race across the meadow, the males displaying their impressive crests and vibrant plumage. I can still hear the wind whistling through the trees and the clinking of the chimes above the swing, coupled with the singing brook and the songs of the birds. The sounds were reminiscent of Beethoven's Sixth Symphony, the *Pastoral,* a perfect soundtrack for what nature provided without any effort. Across the front lawn I would see the rhododendrons marking the entrance to the cabin. Wild flowers grew along the roadside and shared space with the grasshoppers, beetles, and assorted butterflies that covered the terrain. There were daffodils on the hill across the road and impatiens surrounding the front porch, mixed in with gladiolas and peonies, when they were in bloom. A one-hundred-year-old apple tree stood leaning over like an old man, adjacent to the porch, bearing down, heavy with too many apples spilling onto the ground, waiting until winter for the deer to come and feast on them. I stockpiled pictures in the windows of my mind of that cabin, and none of those memories shall ever be forgotten. It was there, by that pond on the other side of the road that I had a profound, spiritual awakening. I still dream about it. If there is such a thing as a past life, it is certain I had lived in that cabin before I was born into this lifetime.

We would celebrate Thanksgiving every year at the cabin in the glen. The girls and I would create recipes and prepare a traditional holiday menu that outshined the previous year, which none of us thought possible. The cabin was too tiny to host a sit-down dinner on a standard dining room table, so we spread the food onto a mahogany, drop-leaf antique table covered with an old Victorian lace tablecloth acquired at a flea market. The scent of the turkey and trimmings, coupled with the wooden logs burning in the old stone fireplace would arouse our appetites. "Ooohs" and "awwws," moans and "mmmms" would blend with sounds of the *Nutcracker Suite* as we each found a place to sit, choosing either the braided throw rug that partially covered the knotty pine floor, the stairwell, the sofa or the upholstered orange, corduroy rocking chairs. The kids and I would gather round that old stone fireplace, savoring the blended aromas of the burning wood logs, while we smacked our lips and enjoyed what we all thought was the best of all possible Thanksgiving dinners. With the exception of the music, the only audible sounds that were heard were the "ughs and ohhhs," lamentations of having overeaten, after we consumed at least two portions of everything and had stuffed our bellies until we could hardly breathe, cherishing every morsel of food and every moment shared together.

The best times of Pam's life were there, during those Thanksgivings in the cabin. It was there she would orchestrate our family sessions, clearing out old cobwebs, hurts and pain that had been accrued by each of us unwittingly over the course of the year. She took on the task of cleaning up the polluted space that interfered with the quality of our family relationships. She conducted family therapy, using her honed, therapeutic skills, weaving a process with clarity, sensitivity, and safety that compelled us to look at ourselves openly and honestly. A wizard therapist, she was able to help us claim our own stuff, without shame or judgment, thereby cleaning up any contaminated space between one another. After the tears and apologies came the hugs and kisses that put everything behind us. The level of intimacy would rise as she restored our sense of togetherness, our bonds and paved the way for the year that would follow. Pam was the engine of the "fabulous five," the others would say. She would lead us into a deeper place of trust, bringing us all to our essence, where time stood still.

Several times a year Pam and I would cofacilitate a retreat for a weekend at the cabin. We would reserve a local lodge for housing, holding our sessions in the cabin. We would each invite our own clients from our respective practices, hers from Los Angeles and mine from South Florida. We witnessed transformation over the three days that would change lives forever. Pam drew the lightening to herself to compel our clients to break down defenses that were keeping them stuck. The cabin in the glen provided the perfect environment for change work, coupled with our skills and resources as therapists. It was during those retreats that we would heal the wounds and traumas of childhood sufferings. We, as mother and daughter and highly trained professionals, worked effectively together to exemplify a healthy relationship. Our efforts and commitment nurtured what they had been missing all of their lives.

It is often said we should have no regrets by the time we reach my age, seventy-four; yet I do. Giving up that cabin is perhaps the only regret in my life. It was there, in that cabin, that Pami was the happiest that I had ever seen her. It was in that cabin that she sang, danced, shared time with her siblings, healed her clients, and found joy with the promise to stay alive. But, as we all know, there are no guarantees in life. Time and change are inexorable. I lost the cabin, yet worst of all, I lost my daughter.

EPILOGUE

Many have consoled us with "There's a reason for everything" and "Sometimes we don't really know why until time passes, or may never know it." How often I have heard others, as well as myself, say, "It was her destiny." I always thought of these phrases as a rationalization to the experience of loss, and a way to understand what is often beyond our capability to comprehend and reconcile.

Sometime in March 2005, a friend told me about a medium who contacts people from the other side. David had recently lost his young wife and had learned of Patrick Matthews through his sister-in-law. He shared his experience of the session with me, urging me to make an appointment. I shrugged it off as some kind of hocus-pocus and forgot about it. A few months passed and he asked if I had made an appointment. Once again I begged off, politely expressing that I really didn't believe in this concept and was wary of metaphysics. Unaffected by my reticence, he encouraged me to follow through. After some deliberation and conscious processing, much to my chagrin I made the call. I was not able to secure a date until October 1, 2005. I was surprised, not only because of how long it took to book the date, but that of all days it was Pam's birthday.

Months passed, and I put it out of my mind until just prior to the appointment. I received an e-mail reminder of the date, time, and telephone number to call. I placed the printed sheet where I would not forget. The next morning I made the call.

The session began promptly, and when it ended I had the resolution that I had always prayed for: Pam had not jumped from fear of the Devil, nor did she jump at her grandparents' invitation to join them in heaven. Her soul had died before her physical body; therefore, her leaping was the consummation of her death. I was told that she did not know what had happened, only that she went from being in her father's apartment to being in heaven. She does not recall the jump or any premeditation of deciding such an act.

When asked if she would be returning to us again, I was told that she had no need, that she was now giving back to us what we had done for her. This was her mission, and she would welcome and receive us when we enter the kingdom of heaven.

I further learned that the Devil cannot take a soul unless it's given. The illness she suffered created "scary" movies in her head that were not true. The truth is that this was God's plan for her.

I was asked to look for a picture in the room where I was sitting during the telephone session. I was told that I would find a picture hanging crooked. This was a sign to let me know she had

been present and would always be with me as well as the other
family members and that there is no separation, even in death.
All the while I was focused on writing down whatever information I was receiving, unaware of my surroundings. On the wall
to my left hangs a picture of a woman who represents "a woman
of valor." On the Sabbath, it is customary to say a prayer to the
woman who prepared the Sabbath dinner, the wife and mother of
the house, honoring her with a blessing. I glanced over and saw
that the picture was indeed crooked. Just before the session ended,
I was asked to think of a sign or symbol that would validate her
presence. Our family always thought of Pam as a butterfly. I had
used this form to acknowledge her presence previously, so I chose
a butterfly. I also used a feather as a symbol, perhaps because of
the feather used in the movie *Forrest Gump*.

I thanked Mr. Matthews for allowing me to learn what I had
yearned to know. I felt peaceful and a sense of serenity filled my
heart.

Upon hanging up, I went over to the wall where the crooked
picture hung, straightened it, smiled, and thanked Pami for vali-
dating her presence.

I had a hair appointment scheduled that same afternoon. During a brief conversation with a friend during that appointment, I
disclosed my morning session with Mr. Matthews. I told her about
the signs, the butterfly and feather, that I had not seen either. I
didn't expect to either as it had been raining most of the day. Right
then I glanced to my left and saw a statue of the Buddha resting

on a decorative gold leaf table in the shape of a feather. There it was, right before my eyes, a larger-than-life feather; I couldn't miss it, even if I tried. I felt elated. Once again, she announced herself.

Later that day, my son Aaron and daughter Erika had been visiting Disney World with their spouses and children. As they entered the park, a small white butterfly greeted them. They were unaware of my conversation earlier that day. Simultaneously, in North Carolina, my other daughter, Monica, was picnicking with her friends. Her boyfriend's little boy, Julian, discovered a feather next to their blanket and innocently presented it to her as a child might offer a flower. Instantly, Monica recognized the significance. As they were preparing to leave, she reached down to fold the blanket, and there perched with its wings fluttering, clinging to the surface was a large black butterfly. At the cemetery alone while visiting his sister, Todd said a prayer and noticed a yellow butterfly hovering over his sister's grave, dancing in the wind.

As I close this book, I will put this all behind me, recalling memories as I choose. I am grateful to the universe for its gifts and the greater understanding it has given me. I am grateful that I could take something so horrific and turn it into a healing experience. And if it helps even one person who has suffered the pain and anguish of living with and/or losing of a loved one, then it was worth all my effort.

ABOUT THE AUTHOR

Joan E. Childs, LCSW, has been in private practice since 1978. She is a Clinical Social Worker specializing in couple's therapy, known as encounter-centered couples therapy certified by Hedy Schliefer, LMFC. Joan is an expert in Codependency, Inner Child Work, Original Pain Work and Second Stage Recovery. She is certified in many modalities including NLP (neuro-linguistic programming), EMDR, (eye movement desensitization and reprocessing), Supervision, Hypnosis, PAIRS, (Practical Applications for Intimate Relationship Skills), and is a Certified Grief Counselor. She was the first affiliate of the John Bradshaw Center in the United States and has appeared on many national television shows including *The Oprah Winfrey Show*.

Joan provides lectures, workshops and seminars dedicated to her profession of mental health and women's issues. She is a spokesperson for bipolar disorder and suicide.

She is the author of *The Myth of the Maiden: On Being a Woman* (1995), published by Health Communications, Inc. Joan had her own television series, *SOLUTIONS*, dedicated to the memory of her daughter, Pam, which offers information and resources for anyone suffering from mental and mood disorders. She is the founder of the Pamela Ann Glassman Educational Center, in cooperation with the Mental Health Center of Broward County.

Joan lives in Hollywood, Florida, and practices in Fort Lauderdale and Hallandale, Florida. You can contact her on her Web site: *www.joanechilds.com*